Martha
Stewart's
Healthy
Quick Cook

Martha Stewart's Healthy

FOUR SEASONS OF GREAT MENUS TO MAKE EVERY DAY

Quick Cook

PHOTOGRAPHS BY JAMES MERRELL

Clarkson Potter/Publishers
New York

To

Alexis Stewart and John Cuti

"Recipes to Share"

Copyright © 1997 by Martha Stewart
Photographs copyright © 1997 by James Merrell

All rights reserved. No part of this book may be reproduced or transmitted in any form or by any means,
electronic or mechanical, including photocopying, recording, or by any information storage and retrieval system,
without permission in writing from the publisher.

Published by Clarkson N. Potter, Inc., 201 East 50th Street,
New York, New York 10022. Member of the Crown Publishing Group.

Random House, Inc. New York, Toronto, London, Sydney, Auckland
http://www.randomhouse.com/

CLARKSON POTTER, POTTER, and colophon are trademarks of Clarkson N. Potter, Inc.

Printed in Japan
Design by Claudia Bruno

Library of Congress Cataloging-in-Publication Data
Stewart, Martha.
Martha Stewart's healthy quick cook/by Martha Stewart.
Includes index.
1. Cookery. 2. Low-fat diet–Recipes. I. Title.
TX714.S781523 1996
641.5'638–dc20 96-31766
ISBN 0-517-57702-X

10 9 8 7 6 5 4 3 2 1

First Edition

ACKNOWLEDGMENTS

A book like this requires the help and in put of a great many people, and I would like to thank everyone who worked on the project. This is the first of my books to be produced under the auspices of my new company, Martha Stewart Living Omnimedia. Susan Spungen, Frances Boswell, and Rori Spinelli from the Martha Stewart Living kitchens led the group of cooks, and Ayesha Patel supervised the stylists who worked on the development, testing, and styling of the food. This group included Cliff Steinert, Wendy Sidewater, Necy Fernandes, and Eric Robledo.

Kathleen Hackett, the Books Editor of Martha Stewart Living, is my editor, and she did a wonderful job collecting information, collating, and editing. Claudia Bruno, an art director at the magazine, designed the book, using the beautiful photographs of James Merrell, an Englishman who spent several long weeks at Westport and East Hampton capturing the visual essence of what we cooked. Grateful thanks also to Laurie Cearley, Joelle Holverson, Laurie Hulston, Kate Edelbaum, Jackie Bobrow, Kim Fasting, Anthony Coombs, Maria Kourebanas, and Mary Ann Young, and my household staff who worked tirelessly during the photography and recipe testing. And many thanks to my longtime friends at Clarkson Potter and Crown, Alberto Vitale, Chip Gibson, Lauren Shakely, Mark McCauslin, Merri Ann Morrell, Jane Treuhaft, Laurie Stark, and Teresa Nicholas, for their continued support and goodwill.

CONTENTS

FALL

WINTER

INTRODUCTION

So much has happened in the world of food and in my cooking and eating habits since I wrote *Quick Cook*, *Quick Cook Menus*, and *Menus for Entertaining*. I still use many of those recipes and love the results, but things change and this book is a reflection of how much things change. I still use butter and oils, and I still eat meats, fish, milk, and eggs. However, I eat more sparingly of rich ingredients and cook with a lighter but equally flavorful touch. **I rely on homemade stocks,** fresh-picked herbs, impeccable vegetables, beautiful ripe fruits, and pure ingredients. Rarely do I open a can, and when I do it is for something foreign or something convenient—like precooked beans. • Asian influences and ingredients and the cuisines of Japan, China, Vietnam, and Thailand now are very important to me, and I often choose dishes from those countries to enliven my meals with exotic tastes and unusual flavors. I love **the taste of fresh cilantro,** delicate tofu, soba and udon noodles, and wasabi. Spices, such as strong curry and tandoori, hot peppers, and **highly flavored mushrooms** are much more important to me than sugar or butter or cream. Flavors can be strong, but for me they must also be delicate. Heavy smoked foods are of little interest, and I much prefer tender flavors like the hot smoked salmon flavored with rosemary and dill or the curried seafood bouillabaisse scented with cardamom, cinnamon, and cloves. I have been very influenced by the cooking of what we call "fusion" chefs, those men and women who are classically trained but who are not afraid to interject **foreign tastes and techniques** into their artful preparations—among these are Nobu Matsuhisa, Alain Ducasse, Jean-Georges Vongerichten, and Daniel Boulud. I am also grateful and indebted to the extremely talented group of young chefs who work tirelessly in the kitchens of my magazine and who introduce me to extraordinary tastes and flavors and **textures and presentations** daily. And, in addition, I am so lucky to travel to unusual places all over the world where my curiosity is sated and my repertoire of ingredients and cooking techniques is enlarged and expanded. A recent trip to the islands in southwestern Japan taught me about the making of udon noodles, and I learned the proper method of opening and serving fresh uni or sea urchin. • What surprises me the most, however, in my every-growing search for the new and the different, **for the healthy and the healthiest,** is the realization that oftentimes the oldest traditions, the antique varieties of fruits and vegetables, and timeworn techniques can still be the best. And I am encouraged that there is still so much to learn, to adapt, and to discover that can help us in our quest for healthy living. • I do hope that you enjoy these recipes as much as we enjoyed creating them for you and that many of them will become your favorites as they have become ours. **Enjoy, Martha**

My pantry has changed quite a bit over the last nine years since I wrote *Quick Cook Menus*. These changes reflect not only my eating habits but the extraordinary influx of unusual and exotic foodstuffs available in American markets. Where once we had to search for wasabi, it is now found in supermarkets; brown basmati rice, a rarity even three years ago, is now a common staple. The "fusion" style of cooking, which incorporates some of the most inventive, unusual, beautiful, delicious, and carefully executed elements of the world's cuisines, has further enhanced the contents of the pantry. Even the layperson is becoming educated in the difference between Arborio and Japanese sweet rice and, blindfolded, can tell balsamic vinegar from sherry wine vinegar. These changes and influences have had a

profound impact on our palates as well as on our pantry. By having an assortment of these excellent and strange ingredients on hand, our everyday cooking and eating can incorporate the healthy with the exotic and the delicious with the nutritious. Here's a list of some key ingredients that will enable you to prepare the recipes in this book: somen noodles, brown basmati rice, quinoa, anchovies, broth (chicken, vegetable, beef), posole, seaweed, sushi nori, cooking wine, Arborio rice, soba noodles, Kokuho Rose rice, couscous, Pernod, wasabi, Aceto Antiqua, black and white peppercorns, dried apricots, canned tomatoes, capers, rigatoni (and other pastas), an assortment of dried spices and herbs, flavored vinegars, extra-virgin olive oil, dried and canned beans, assorted lentils, and white wine.

BASICS

Chicken Stock

5   *pounds chicken bones*
1   *large onion, peeled and quartered*
1   *large carrot, cut into thirds*
2   *celery stalks, cut into thirds*
2   *large or 4 small leeks, cut in half*
     lengthwise and well washed
2   *bay leaves*
6   *sprigs of fresh flat-leaf parsley*
1/2 *teaspoon dried thyme*
12 *whole black peppercorns*

MAKES 1 1/2 QUARTS

Place all the ingredients in an 8-quart stock pot and cover with cold water. Bring to a boil over high heat. As the stock approaches a boil, remove any impurities that rise to the top by skimming with a ladle. Reduce the heat and simmer the stock for 3 to 4 hours, continuing to skim impurities from time to time while the stock cooks. Taste after 3 hours for the strength of stock you want. Remove from the heat and let the stock sit for 10 to 15 minutes, then ladle through a fine strainer. Once strained, remove the fat from the stock by skimming with a ladle (see Note). Cool by placing the container of strained stock in an ice water bath, then refrigerate.

The stock will keep for about 1 week in the refrigerator, or freeze in 1-cup batches.

Note: Another way to defat the stock is to place the cooled stock in the refrigerator overnight. The fat will set on the top and can be easily spooned off.

Variation: Use a large (5- to 6-pound) roasting chicken in place of the bones. Use the meat for chicken salad or croquettes.

Vegetable Stock

3   *cups mushrooms (any variety)*
1   *fennel bulb, stalks and leaves only*
     (reserve the bulb for another use)
5   *celery stalks*
4   *medium to large carrots*
2   *large onions*
1/4 *head of green cabbage*
1/2 *large rutabaga, peeled*
5   *leeks, cut in half lengthwise and washed*
1   *small bunch of fresh flat-leaf parsley*
     (about 15 sprigs)
1   *head of garlic, cut in half crosswise to*
     expose the cloves
12 *whole black peppercorns*
6   *whole white peppercorns*
3   *bay leaves*
6–8 *sprigs of fresh thyme*

MAKES 2 QUARTS

Slice the mushrooms, fennel stalks, celery, carrots, onions, and cabbage thin and place in an 8-quart stockpot. Cut the rutabaga into large chunks and place in the stockpot. Add the remaining ingredients and cover with cold water.

Bring to a boil over high heat. As the stock approaches a boil, skim any impurities that rise to the top with a ladle. Lower the heat and simmer gently for 45 to 60 minutes. Remove from the heat and cool for 10 to 15 minutes. Ladle through a fine strainer, cool, and refrigerate. The stock will keep for 4 to 5 days in the refrigerator, or freeze in 1-cup batches.

Note: To intensify the flavor, reduce the stock after straining by one quarter to one half.

Shellfish Stock

1 1/2 *teaspoons extra-virgin olive oil*
3–4 *lobster heads (tail and claws*
     removed), cut in 3 or 4 pieces
     (see Note)
3   *tablespoons Cognac*
2   *plum tomatoes, sliced*
1   *tablespoon tomato paste*
2   *large or 4 small leeks, cut in half length-*
     wise and washed well
1   *medium-size onion, sliced*
2   *celery stalks, cut in half*
1   *head of garlic, cut across the middle to*
     expose the cloves
6   *sprigs of fresh flat-leaf parsley*
2   *bay leaves*
12 *whole black peppercorns*
6   *sprigs of fresh thyme*
3   *sprigs of fresh tarragon*

MAKES 1 1/2 QUARTS

Heat an 8-quart stockpot over high heat for about 2 minutes. Add the olive oil and lobster and sauté until the shells turn bright red. Remove the pan from the heat, add the Cognac, then return to the heat and allow the alcohol to burn off, about 15 to 20 seconds. Add the tomatoes and tomato paste and stir. Add the remaining ingredients and cover with cold water. Bring to a boil over high heat, skim, and reduce the heat. Simmer gently for 1 to 1 1/2 hours. Cool slightly and strain through a fine sieve.

The stock will keep for 2 to 3 days in the refrigerator, or freeze in 1-cup batches.

Note: You can substitute shrimp shells for the lobster heads. The more you use, the richer the stock will be. When cooking shrimp or lobsters, simply reserve the shells or heads as the case may be and freeze them so you will have them available to prepare this stock.

Beef Stock

3   pounds beef shank bones, cut into
      2-inch pieces
4   lean short ribs of beef
4   leeks, cut into half lengthwise and
      washed
4   celery stalks
2   whole carrots, peeled
1   yellow onion, unpeeled and halved
3   fresh bay leaves
1   large sprig of fresh thyme
2   white spring onions, trimmed
      Handful of fresh flat-leaf parsley
1   whole head of garlic, unpeeled
½   teaspoon whole black peppercorns

MAKES 3 CUPS

Preheat the oven to 400°F. Place all of the ingredients in an 8-quart Dutch oven. Add 2 cups of water and roast in the oven for 30 minutes.

Remove the pot from the oven and add water to cover. Simmer on top of the stove for 3 to 4 hours. Let the stock cool slightly, skim off any fat, and strain, reserving the beef bones for serving simply with strong horseradish. Refrigerate, or freeze the stock in smaller amounts for future use.

Lamb Stock

1½   pounds lamb bones
1   medium-size onion, peeled and pierced
      with 1 whole clove
1   carrot, peeled
½   cup fresh celery leaves
½   cup parsley stems
1   garlic clove, peeled
1   teaspoon kosher salt
8   whole black peppercorns
1   fresh thyme sprig

MAKES 5 CUPS

In a stockpot, combine the lamb bones with about 12 cups of cold water, or enough to cover.

Bring the mixture to a boil and skim off the froth. Add the remaining ingredients and simmer over low heat, covered partially, for 2 hours. Strain the broth through a sieve, discarding the bones and the vegetables. Allow the stock to cool. Chill the stock in the refrigerator and skim off the fat. The stock can be frozen for up to 2 months.

Lemon Dill Yogurt Sauce

½   cup nonfat plain yogurt
½   teaspoon minced garlic
2   teaspoons chopped capers
2   teaspoons fresh lemon juice
2   teaspoons chopped fresh dill

MAKES ½ CUP

In a small bowl, stir together all of the ingredients. Refrigerate until ready to serve. This yogurt sauce should be used on the day that it is made.

Roasted Garlic

3–4 garlic heads

MAKES ABOUT ½ CUP PURÉE

Preheat the oven to 425°F.

Place the garlic heads in a baking dish. Bake until soft, approximately 30 minutes. Let the garlic cool, and then squeeze out the pulp. Alternatively, store the whole garlic heads, tightly covered, in the refrigerator for up to 10 days.

Rough-Cut Basil Pesto

½   cup coarsely chopped basil
2   teaspoons extra-virgin olive oil
1   teaspoon Roasted Garlic (above)
      Kosher salt and freshly ground black
      pepper

MAKES ½ CUP

In a bowl, combine the basil, oil, garlic, and salt and pepper, and mash together with the back of a fork. The pesto will keep, tightly covered, in the refrigerator for 2 days.

Enlightened Crème Fraîche

½   cup buttermilk
½   cup heavy cream

MAKES 1 CUP

Combine the ingredients in a plastic container. Set the mixture aside in a warm place for 24 to 36 hours, until thickened. Refrigerate immediately. Whip until thickened before serving. This will keep, tightly covered, for about 4 days in the refrigerator.

Note: This "enlightened" version of crème fraîche has a higher ratio of low-fat buttermilk to high-fat cream.

Soy Dipping Sauce

¼   cup light soy sauce
2   tablespoons rice vinegar
¾   teaspoon sesame oil
1   tablespoon plus 1 teaspoon water
1   teaspoon grated fresh ginger
2   teaspoons chopped garlic

MAKES ½ CUP

Combine all the ingredients in a small bowl and mix well. Serve in individual dipping bowls with any dumpling or roll, or with steamed vegetables.

Yogurt Cheese

1   *cup low-fat plain yogurt*

MAKES ¼ CUP

Set a colander over a bowl and line the colander with a layer of paper towels or coffee filters. Pour the yogurt into the colander and chill, covered, for about 2 hours, or until thick.

Red Pepper Coulis

3   *red bell peppers*
2   *teaspoons balsamic vinegar*
    Kosher salt

MAKES ABOUT 1 CUP

Preheat the oven to 425°F.

Place the peppers in a roasting pan and roast, turning every 15 minutes, for 45 minutes, until the skins are wrinkled and slightly charred.

Transfer the peppers to a cooling rack. When cool enough to handle, peel the peppers over a bowl, allowing the juices to collect in the bowl. Discard the skins. Combine the peppers, collected juices, and balsamic vinegar in a food processor and process until smooth. Season with salt.

The coulis will keep, tightly covered, in the refrigerator for up to 3 days.

Note: For a finer sauce, strain the purée through a strainer, pushing it with a wooden spoon.

Dulce de Leche

½   *cup nonfat sweetened condensed milk*
2   *tablespoons sugar*

MAKES ¼ CUP

In a small saucepan, combine the milk and sugar and cook over medium heat until reduced by half, about 10 minutes. The mixture will turn the color of peanut shells.

Arugula Pesto

1   *large bunch of arugula, trimmed and coarsely chopped (about 1 packed cup)*
2   *tablespoons extra-virgin olive oil*
1   *small garlic clove, minced*
2   *teaspoons lemon juice*
    Kosher salt and freshly ground black pepper

MAKES ¾ CUP

Combine all of the ingredients and mash together with a fork. Serve immediately.

Buttermilk Dressing

3   *tablespoons extra-virgin olive oil*
2   *tablespoons lemon juice*
5   *tablespoons buttermilk*
2   *tablespoons coarsely chopped parsley*

MAKES ¾ CUP

In a small bowl, whisk together the olive oil and lemon juice. Whisk in the buttermilk and parsley. The dressing will keep, covered, in the refrigerator for 3 days.

Warm Apple Thyme Dressing

⅔   *cup apple cider*
1   *apple, finely chopped*
2   *tablespoons lemon juice*
1   *tablespoon extra-virgin olive oil*
½   *teaspoon fresh oregano*
½   *teaspoon fresh thyme*

MAKES ¾ CUP

Combine all of the ingredients in a small saucepan and boil for 3 to 5 minutes, until the juices are slightly thickened and the apples are soft but not broken down. The dressing will keep, tightly covered, in the refrigerator for 3 days.

Pineapple Cranberry Chutney

2   *tablespoons olive oil*
1   *shallot, thinly sliced into rings*
1   *medium pineapple, trimmed and cut into cubes (about 4 cups)*
¼   *cup sugar*
½   *cup pineapple juice*
1   *tablespoon balsamic vinegar*
1   *cup fresh or frozen cranberries*
2   *tablespoons fresh thyme*

MAKES 1½ CUPS

In a saucepan over medium heat, combine the oil and shallot and cook until the shallot rings are translucent, about 5 minutes. Add the pineapple and sugar and cook, stirring to coat the pineapple with the sugar, until the sugar is dissolved and the pineapple begins to soften. Add ¼ cup of the pineapple juice and the balsamic vinegar and cook until the liquid is reduced by half, about 5 to 7 minutes. Add the remaining juice and cranberries and cook until the cranberries pop and the juice thickens, about 3 to 5 minutes. Stir in the thyme and serve. The chutney will keep, tightly covered, in the refrigerator up to one week.

Raw Yellow Pepper Vinaigrette

1   *large yellow bell pepper, finely chopped*
     (about 1 cup)
4   *teaspoons red wine vinegar*
     Kosher salt and freshly ground black
     pepper to taste
2   *tablespoons extra-virgin olive oil*
2   *teaspoons warm water*
     Pinch of sugar

MAKES 1 CUP

In a medium bowl, whisk together all of the ingredients until combined well. The vinaigrette will keep, tightly covered, in the refrigerator for about 3 days.

Dill Shallot Vinaigrette

1   *large shallot, minced (about*
     2 tablespoons)
¼   *cup minced fresh dill*
2   *tablespoons red wine vinegar*
2   *teaspoons balsamic vinegar*
1   *tablespoon water*
     Kosher salt to taste
1½ *tablespoons extra-virgin olive oil*

MAKES ½ CUP

In a small bowl, whisk together all of the ingredients except the oil. Slowly add the oil, whisking vigorously, until the vinaigrette is emulsified. Store, tightly covered, in the refrigerator for up to 8 hours.

Note: Use this recipe as a guide for making other flavorful, lower fat vinaigrettes. Basil, thyme, tarragon—almost any fresh herb works well here.

Red Pepper Vinaigrette

½   *cup Red Pepper Coulis (page 15)*
2   *tablespoons red wine vinegar*
     Kosher salt and freshly ground black
     pepper
½   *cup extra-virgin olive oil*

MAKES ¾ CUP

Whisk the coulis, vinegar, and salt and pepper together in a medium bowl. Slowly add the oil, whisking vigorously, until the vinaigrette is emulsified. This will keep, tightly covered, in the refrigerator for about 1 week.

Tarragon Vinaigrette

½   *cup fresh lemon juice*
¼   *cup extra-virgin olive oil*
     Kosher salt and freshly ground black
     pepper
4   *tablespoons whole fresh tarragon leaves,*
     cut into thirds

MAKES ¾ CUP

In a small bowl, whisk together the lemon juice and oil until well blended. Season with salt and pepper. Just before serving, stir in the tarragon. Serve this vinaigrette on the day it is made.

Sesame Vinaigrette

¼	cup rice vinegar
1	tablespoon clover honey
¼	cup sesame oil
2	tablespoons roasted peanut oil
2	tablespoons canola oil
	Kosher salt and freshly ground black pepper
1	tablespoon boiling water
2	tablespoons sesame seeds

MAKES ¾ CUP

Place all ingredients except the water and sesame seeds in the bowl of a small food processor and process for 30 seconds. Add the boiling water and process for an additional 10 to 15 seconds. Stir in the sesame seeds. The vinaigrette will keep, tightly covered, in the refrigerator for about 1 week.

Citrus Vinaigrette

1	teaspoon white wine vinegar
1	tablespoon lemon juice
1	tablespoon honey
½	cup grapefruit juice
2	tablespoons canola oil
1	large grapefruit, peeled, pith removed and cut into sections
	Kosher salt and freshly ground black pepper

MAKES ¾ CUP

In a small bowl, whisk together the vinegar, lemon juice, honey, grapefruit juice, and canola oil. Add the grapefruit sections and season with salt and pepper. The vinaigrette will keep, tightly covered, in the refrigerator for up to 3 days.

Jalapeño Vinaigrette

3	jalapeño peppers
1	tablespoon coarsely chopped cilantro
1	tablespoon coarsely chopped shallots
2	tablespoons fresh lemon juice
	Kosher salt and freshly ground black pepper
3	tablespoons extra-virgin olive oil

MAKES ¾ CUP

In a nonstick saucepan, roast the jalapeños over high heat until the skins char. Turn the heat off, cover the pan, and set aside for 5 minutes. Peel the cooled jalapeños and remove the stems. Slice lengthwise and, over a small bowl, scrape out the seeds and discard while allowing the juices to collect in the bowl. Add the cilantro, shallots, lemon juice, and salt and pepper to the bowl and whisk to combine. Whisk in the olive oil. The vinaigrette will keep, tightly covered, in the refrigerator for 2 days.

Lime Caper Vinaigrette

2	tablespoons extra-virgin olive oil
¼	cup fresh lime juice
¼	cup finely chopped fresh parsley
2	dashes of Tabasco sauce
2	teaspoons capers
½	teaspoon dried hot red pepper flakes
	Kosher salt and freshly ground black pepper
1	teaspoon sugar

MAKES 1 CUP

In a small bowl, whisk together the olive oil, lemon juice, parsley, 1 tablespoon of water, and Tabasco. Stir in the capers, red pepper flakes, salt, pepper, and sugar. The vinaigrette will keep, tightly covered, in the refrigerator for up to 2 days.

Orange Vinaigrette

¼	cup fresh orange juice
¼	cup lemon juice
	Kosher salt and freshly ground pepper
2	tablespoons extra-virgin olive oil
2	tablespoons canola oil

MAKES ¾ CUP

Combine the juices and salt and pepper. Slowly whisk in the oils until incorporated. The vinaigrette will keep, tightly covered, in the refrigerator for 2 days.

Chive Vinaigrette

¼	cup minced chives
2	tablespoons white wine vinegar
1	tablespoon Dijon mustard
1	tablespoon water
2	teaspoons honey
	Kosher salt and freshly ground pepper
4	teaspoons extra-virgin olive oil

MAKES ½ CUP

In a small bowl, whisk together all the ingredients except the oil. Slowly add the oil, whisking vigorously, until the vinaigrette is emulsified. The vinaigrette will keep, tightly covered, in the refrigerator for up to 2 days.

Poppy Seed Vinaigrette

1	tablespoon lemon juice
1	tablespoon balsamic vinegar
4	tablespoons extra-virgin olive oil
	Kosher salt and freshly ground pepper
1	tablespoon poppy seeds

MAKES ¾ CUP

In a small bowl, whisk together the lemon juice and vinegar. Add the olive oil drop by drop, whisking constantly. Season with salt and pepper. Whisk in poppy seeds. The vinaigrette will keep, tightly covered, in the refrigerator for up to 2 days.

SPRING

As a gardener, I can barely wait for that day when I sow my first seeds in the vegetable garden. Each year I read my seed catalogs with great interest: What is new? What haven't I tried before? What can I not live without? I order my seeds—sometimes every available variety of a vegetable or herb, like basil, to see what the differences in taste really are. Last year, I grew every kind of mesclun mix—combinations of salad greens and herbs, which, depending on the region they come from, are spicy, pungent, mild, or tender. This year I grew almost every kind of garlic, again, as an experiment in flavor differentiation. And I await with pleasure the picking of my homegrown horseradish this autumn. Springtime is the best time of year to indulge in the art of "foraging"—or searching for those unique and amazing foodstuffs that contribute to the new style of "haute cuisine," which is fresh, elegant, uncomplicated, and experimental. The amazing ramp, the purple artichoke, the deepest red or palest pink rhubarb stalks, and the freshly picked chanterelle or morel make up a palette that the springtime cook can delight in. Everything fits perfectly into a regimen of healthy cooking and healthy eating. The Asian tradition of stir-frying and steaming respects the most delicate of ingredients, and quick grilling and pan searing seal in flavors while maintaining the fragile qualities of the newly harvested items that make each of the following menus special.

MENU · GRILLED SCALLOPS WITH SPRING GREENS · LEMON RISOTTO · STEWED RHUBARB AND RASPBERRIES WITH A MERINGUE LATTICE CRUST · SERVES 4

One of the best ways to prepare sea scallops is one of the easiest—seasoned simply with salt and pepper and grilled to sweet, smoky perfection. The best way to eat them is on a bed of tender lettuces and soft herbs such as basil and mint and very lightly dressed or even undressed—the juicy scallops perfuming the greens ever so slightly. Traditionally served as a first course in Italy, risotto is most often a main course here, but I like to serve this Lemon Risotto in a warmed serving dish and spoon it onto warmed side plates. In order to make fast work of this menu, prepare the ingredients for each recipe first—chop the rhubarb for the dessert, wash and dice the leek, zest the lemon, etc. Make dessert first, then grill the scallops and make the dressing for the greens. Because risotto should always be served immediately, prepare it last.

Grilled Scallops with Spring Greens

12	large sea scallops
	Kosher salt and freshly ground black pepper
½	teaspoon herbed Dijon mustard
1	teaspoon sherry vinegar
1	teaspoon fresh lemon juice
1	tablespoon extra-virgin olive oil
1	teaspoon walnut oil
1	teaspoon boiling water
4	cups mixed greens (baby spinach, arugula, mâche)
¼	cup coarsely chopped basil leaves
1	teaspoon chopped fresh tarragon
4	6-inch bamboo skewers soaked in water

SERVES 4

Spray a ridged cast-iron stove-top griddle or outdoor grill with nonstick cooking spray and preheat it. Season the scallops lightly with salt and pepper, thread 3 on each of the skewers, and grill about 1½ minutes per side, or until slightly firm. Remove and set aside.

Meanwhile, place the mustard, vinegar, lemon juice, and a pinch of salt and pepper in a small food processor. With the machine running, add the oils in a stream. Process for about 30 seconds, then add the boiling water and process for about 10 seconds more.

Mix the lettuces with the herbs and the dressing, reserving about 2 teaspoons of dressing. Divide the lettuces evenly among 4 plates. Arrange 3 scallops on each plate, drizzle with the reserved dressing, and serve.

Lemon Risotto

1	large leek, white part only, well washed and cut into ½-inch dice
1	tablespoon plus 1 teaspoon unsalted butter
1	cup Arborio rice
2	cups Vegetable Stock (page 13) or low-sodium canned
	Kosher salt and freshly ground black pepper
1	tablespoon lemon zest
2	tablespoons lemon juice
2	tablespoons chopped chives

SERVES 4

Sweat the leek in 2 teaspoons of butter over low heat in a tightly covered straight-sided sauté pan for 6 minutes, stirring once or twice. Add the rice and raise the heat to medium, stirring often for 3 minutes. Add 1 cup of stock, season lightly with salt and pepper, and stir until all of the liquid has been absorbed. Add the remaining broth, ½ cup at a time, stirring constantly after each addition. When all of the liquid is absorbed, add the zest and continue to cook for about 10 minutes more, until the rice is al dente. Stir in the lemon juice. Season well with salt and pepper, add the chives, stir in the remaining 2 teaspoons of butter until it melts, and serve hot.

OPPOSITE *My handsome English ironstone square bowl is perfect for piping-hot risotto, studded with the first leeks of spring and brightened with plenty of fresh-squeezed lemon juice.*

Stewed Rhubarb and Raspberries with a Meringue Lattice Crust

1¼ pounds fresh rhubarb (about 6 stalks)
      or 4 cups frozen, cut into 1-inch
      pieces
1   pint fresh raspberries
¾   cup sugar
1   tablespoon all-purpose flour
2   cups Swiss Meringue (recipe follows)

SERVES 4

Combine the rhubarb, raspberries, sugar, and flour in a saucepan and cook over medium heat until the juices thicken, about 5 to 7 minutes. Reduce the heat and simmer for 20 to 30 minutes, until the rhubarb is soft. Transfer to a 4-cup shallow ovenproof baking dish and set aside.

Preheat the oven to 475°F. Make the meringue.

Fill a clean pastry bag fitted with the giant open star tip with the meringue. Pipe out the meringue onto the raspberry mixture into a simple latticework topping. Bake until very lightly browned, about 5 to 7 minutes. Serve immediately.

Swiss Meringue

2   large egg whites, at room temperature
½   cup sugar
      Pinch of cream of tartar
¼   teaspoon pure vanilla extract

MAKES 2 CUPS

Fill a medium saucepan one quarter full with water. Set the saucepan over medium heat and bring the water to a simmer.

Combine the egg whites, sugar, and cream of tartar in the heatproof bowl of an electric mixer and place over the saucepan. Whisk constantly until the sugar is dissolved and the whites are warm to the touch, 3 to 3½ minutes. Test by rubbing between your fingers.

Transfer the bowl to the electric mixer and whip, starting on low speed and gradually increasing to high, until stiff, glossy peaks form, about 10 minutes. Add the vanilla and mix until combined.

ABOVE *Grilled Scallops with Spring Greens announce the season on playful green transferware plates, which complement beautifully my two-color Depression glass stemware.* **RIGHT** *A very simple meringue lattice crust floats atop a flavorful stew of raspberries and rhubarb.*

MENU · ENDIVE, ARUGULA, AND TANGERINE SALAD · GRILLED TUNA STEAK · COUSCOUS WITH GREEN AND WHITE ASPARAGUS · ESPRESSO ICE MILK · SERVES 4

Grilled fish of any kind and a simple salad is among my favorite meals. The quick "marinade" for this Grilled Tuna Steak is pungent enough to subtly infuse the fish within 15 minutes, my solution to overnight marinating. Because it features ingredients with assertive flavors, it is best used on the stronger tuna varieties such as skipjack, tunny, or bonito. I always section citrus—and any other juicy fruits—over a bowl or parchment paper and return the juices that collect to the recipe in some way. Here, the tangerine juices become an ingredient in the vinaigrette for the salad. Delicious Espresso Ice Milk is a snap to pull together but must chill before freezing in an ice cream maker, so you might want to prepare it up to the chilling point in the morning.

Endive, Arugula, and Tangerine Salad

2   heads of Belgian endive, coarsely chopped (about 2 cups)
2   handfuls of arugula, torn into bite-size pieces (about 5 cups)
2   tangerines, peeled, pith removed
4   teaspoons red wine vinegar
2   tablespoons extra-virgin olive oil
    Kosher salt and freshly ground black pepper

SERVES 4

Wash and dry the endive and arugula and place in a serving bowl. Over a small bowl and using a sharp paring knife, carefully remove each section of tangerine, cutting between the membranes. Add the sections to the greens. When all the sections have been removed, squeeze the membranes over the bowl. Whisk in the vinegar and oil and season with salt and pepper. Toss the dressing with the greens and serve.

Grilled Tuna Steak

1   large lemon, zested and juiced (about ¼ cup juice)
6   anchovy fillets, cut into thirds
1   garlic clove, minced
1   tablespoon whole oregano leaves
2   tablespoons whole basil leaves
2   1-inch-thick tuna steaks (about 8 ounces each), cut in half
    Kosher salt and freshly ground black pepper

SERVES 4

Combine the zest, juice, anchovies, garlic, and herbs in a dish. Add the tuna, turn to coat, and marinate for 15 minutes at room temperature or 1 hour in the refrigerator.

Prepare a ridged cast-iron stove-top griddle or outdoor grill. Salt and pepper the tuna and grill until well browned but still rare, about 2 minutes per side; the flesh will be firm and tight. For medium rare, cook 1 minute more, until the flesh begins to pull apart. For medium, cook 2 minutes more, until the flesh flakes apart. Remove to a cutting board to rest.

Meanwhile, bring the marinade to a boil. Arrange the tuna on dinner plates and spoon 2 tablespoons of marinade over each piece.

ABOVE *My collection of English ironstone is perfect for everyday use.* **RIGHT** *Grilled Tuna Steak is dressed in its marinade and accompanied by asparagus-studded couscous.*

ABOVE *A simple side dish in no time: cous-cous is tossed with the very freshest green and white asparagus and tender arugula, then driz-zled with good-quality olive oil.* **OPPOSITE** *The gorgeous color of Espresso Ice Milk is all the more striking in a footed antique glass compote set on a Wedgwood dessert plate.*

Couscous with Green and White Asparagus

1½   cups Chicken Stock (page 13) or
        low-sodium canned, fat skimmed
1   cup couscous
¾   pound green and white asparagus, ends
        trimmed, cut in half (about 2 cups)
        Kosher salt and freshly ground black
        pepper
¼   cup chopped arugula
2   teaspoons extra-virgin olive oil

SERVES 4

In a medium pot, bring the stock to a boil. Add the couscous, stir, and bring to a boil. Remove from the heat.

In a large pot of boiling water, blanch the asparagus and then transfer to a bowl filled with ice water.

Season the couscous with salt and pepper. Stir in asparagus, cover, and let stand 5 minutes. Fluff with a fork and transfer to a bowl. Stir in the arugula and olive oil, season with salt and pepper, and serve.

Espresso Ice Milk

3   cups (2 12-ounce cans) low-fat
        evaporated milk
½   cup sugar
¼   cup brewed espresso
¼   teaspoon pure vanilla extract
⅛   teaspoon kosher salt

MAKES 1 QUART

Heat the evaporated milk in a 2-quart saucepan over low heat until warm.

Stir together the sugar and 2 tablespoons of the espresso in a heavy saucepan. Place over high heat and cook, without stirring, about 2 minutes (the mixture will bubble), until the sugar has caramelized to a dark amber. Remove from the heat and pour in the remaining 2 tablespoons espresso.

Stir the espresso mixture into the warm milk and mix well. Stir in the vanilla and salt. Cover and chill thoroughly.

Freeze in an ice cream maker according to the manufacturer's directions.

MENU · BRIGHT GREEN PEA SOUP ·
PAN-SEARED LOIN OF LAMB · SPOON-MASHED POTATOES ·
CORNMEAL BISCUITS WITH KIWI · SERVES 4

I love this menu, which combines my favorite springtime foods, peas and lamb. It is be perfect for a casual dinner or a big celebration such as Easter or Passover. My simple version of pea soup is inspired by the exquisite, jewel-toned flat and round pea soup served at The Tea Box, one of the most serene cafes in all of Manhattan. To prevent the peas from losing their vibrant color once you've puréed them, the soup must be cooled very quickly.

A sturdy bowl and large spoon are all you need to make my rustic version of mashed potatoes. Don't even think of peeling the potatoes—the skins are flavorful and full of fiber. My cornmeal biscuits recipe makes more dough than you need. Shape the dough in a log, wrap it in plastic, and freeze. Slice and bake the cookies as needed.

Bright Green Pea Soup

2   teaspoons extra-virgin olive oil
2   shallots, peeled and thinly sliced
3   cups Chicken Stock (page 13) or
        Vegetable Stock (page 13) or
        low-sodium canned
3   pounds fresh peas, shelled, or 5 cups frozen
½   cup low-fat plain yogurt
    Kosher salt and freshly ground black pepper
    Fresh tarragon sprigs, for garnish

SERVES 4

In a large soup pot, heat the olive oil over low heat. Add the shallots and cook, covered, until they are soft and translucent. Add the stock and bring to a boil. Reduce the heat and simmer, uncovered, for 10 minutes.

Add the peas and simmer 10 minutes more for fresh peas and 4 minutes for frozen, or until the peas are just heated through and still vibrant. Purée the mixture in a blender and pour through a wide-mesh strainer into a bowl set in a larger bowl filled with ice and cold water. Stir until cool to the touch. Stir in the yogurt and season with salt and pepper. Divide among 4 chilled soup bowls and garnish with sprigs of tarragon.

Pan-Seared Loin of Lamb

1¾ pounds loin of lamb, boned and
        trimmed of fat (about 12 ounces),
        tied with kitchen string, if necessary,
        to form uniform shape
1   tablespoon extra-virgin olive oil
2   large branches of rosemary, stems
        removed and leaves coarsely chopped
        (about ¼ cup)
2   garlic cloves, coarsely chopped
    Kosher salt and freshly ground black pepper
¼   cup good-quality red wine
3   cups Lamb Stock (page 14) or Chicken
        Stock (page 13) or low-sodium canned
1   teaspoon all-purpose flour

SERVES 4

Moisten the loin with 1 teaspoon of olive oil. Combine the rosemary and garlic and rub it into the loin. Season with salt and pepper.

In a large nonstick skillet over medium-high heat, add the remaining oil. Sear the lamb for 8 to 10 minutes on each side, until the meat is firm to the touch and the internal temperature on a meat thermometer is 135°F. Remove the meat to a cutting board to rest for 10 minutes.

Meanwhile, wipe the fat from the skillet with a paper towel. Return the skillet to the heat and add the wine. Cook until the liquid has reduced by half, about 1 minute, scraping the pan with a wooden spoon to loosen the browned bits. Add the stock and simmer until the liquid is reduced by half. Meanwhile, dissolve the flour in ¼ cup of water. Add to the stock and let simmer and thicken, about 1 minute. Season with salt and pepper.

Slice the loin into ½-inch slices and arrange among 4 dinner plates. Spoon the pan juices onto each plate and serve alongside the Spoon-Mashed Potatoes.

OPPOSITE *Bright Green Pea Soup is dazzling in an antique Limoges soup bowl.* **ABOVE** *The most tender cut of all, loin of lamb thinly sliced and drizzled with rosemary-scented pan juices is light yet succulent.*

Spoon-Mashed Potatoes

1   pound baby Red Bliss potatoes
1   teaspoon extra-virgin olive oil
1   teaspoon kosher salt
3   tablespoons low-fat buttermilk
    Freshly ground black pepper

MAKES 2 CUPS

Preheat the oven to 425°F. Combine the potatoes, olive oil, and salt in a 9 × 11-inch roasting pan and toss thoroughly. Roast the potatoes until fork-tender, about 35 to 40 minutes. Transfer to a bowl and, using a wooden spoon, smash the potatoes up against the side of the bowl. Add the buttermilk and continue to smash the potatoes until the liquid is thoroughly combined. Season with the pepper and serve.

Cornmeal Biscuits with Kiwi

2   tablespoons butter
¼   cup sugar, plus 1 teaspoon for
      sprinkling
1   egg yolk
½   cup all-purpose flour
¼   cup cornmeal, plus extra for dusting
¼   teaspoon kosher salt
1   kiwi, peeled and sliced into 4 rounds

MAKES 1 DOZEN COOKIES

In a medium bowl, cream together the butter and ¼ cup sugar until smooth. Add the yolk and mix to combine. In a separate bowl, whisk together the dry ingredients. Add them to the egg mixture and stir just to combine. The mixture will resemble coarse crumbs. Add 1 tablespoon of cold water to bring the dough together. Wrap in plastic and freeze for ½ hour.

Preheat the oven to 350°F. Line a baking sheet with parchment.

Dust the countertop with cornmeal. Using your fingertips, press the dough to a ¼-inch thickness about 8 inches around, and cut into desired shapes. Gently run a knife under each shape to remove and place on a cookie sheet. Sprinkle sparingly with sugar. Bake until golden, about 10 to 12 minutes. Remove the biscuits to a wire rack to cool. Arrange 2 cookies and a slice of kiwi on each of 4 dessert plates. The remaining cookies will keep, tightly covered, for up to 3 days.

ABOVE *White hyacinths infuse the air with the sweet smell of spring.* RIGHT *I always like to end a meal with a "little something," such as these cornmeal biscuits.*

MENU · MUSSELS AND BABY ARTICHOKES BARIGOULE · SPAGHETTI SQUASH WITH SAGE AND ORANGE · FORELLE PEARS IN PARCHMENT · SERVES 4

I love steamed shellfish, especially when paired with another one of my very favorite foods, artichokes. Tiny clams work beautifully in this version of the classic French dish, too. Rather than using ersatz ingredients to achieve full flavor, I would much rather use less of the real thing, as I do here with a very small amount of pancetta. It gives the sauce such a distinctive salty, spicy depth that a substitute simply wouldn't do. I will often toss spaghetti squash in a sturdy sauce, but in this menu I prefer it very clean and lightly seasoned. When prepared this way, it is best to choose smaller spaghetti squash since the strands are more delicate. Use whatever fruits are in season for the dessert. The miniature Forelles have a very short season and I like to use them in as many ways as I can. Crisp, sweet, and pretty, they're just as delicious eaten out of hand.

Mussels and Baby Artichokes Barigoule

12	baby artichokes, trimmed, tough outer leaves removed
1	lemon, cut in half
2	ounces pancetta, cubed
2	teaspoons extra-virgin olive oil
3	medium shallots, peeled and sliced into ¼-inch rings
2	whole garlic cloves, unpeeled
5	medium carrots, sliced into ¼-inch rings
2	large bay leaves
2	sprigs of fresh thyme
1	teaspoon kosher salt, plus more to taste
¼	teaspoon freshly ground black pepper, plus more to taste
½	cup dry white wine
1	cup Chicken Stock (page 13) or low-sodium canned
2	pounds mussels, scrubbed, debearded, and rinsed
½	cup coarsely chopped parsley
1	tablespoon balsamic vinegar

SERVES 4

Neatly pare the base and stem of the artichokes, then cut off the tip. Rub with the lemon and place in acidulated ice water.

In a heavy Dutch oven, cook the pancetta in the olive oil over moderate heat until brown and very crisp, about 10 minutes. Remove the pancetta with a slotted spoon and reserve. Remove all but 1 teaspoon of the rendered fat from the pan and add the shallots and garlic. Cook for 5 minutes, stirring and picking up the brown bits from the bottom of the pan, until golden brown.

Add the carrots, bay leaves, thyme, salt, and pepper to the Dutch oven and cook until just tender, 4 to 6 minutes. Add the wine and stock and stir until it boils. Place the artichokes on the bed of vegetables, cover, and simmer over medium-low heat until tender, 20 to 30 minutes, stirring occasionally. Add the mussels to the Dutch oven 5 to 10 minutes before the artichokes are tender and cook until they have opened. Remove any opened mussels into a large serving bowl or deep platter and cover with foil. Continue cooking the others until they open, about 5 minutes longer. Discard any unopened mussels. If the liquid has evaporated, add ½ cup additional stock. Turn up the heat and reduce the liquid just to thicken slightly and adjust the seasoning with salt and pepper. Stir in the parsley and reserved pancetta. Place the artichokes and any remaining opened mussels in the serving bowl, spoon the vegetables on top, drizzle with balsamic vinegar, and serve.

OPPOSITE *The barigoule is prepared in a deep copper saucepan, handsome enough to transfer from stovetop to dinner table.* **FAR LEFT** *Roasted Spaghetti Squash cool in an antique enamelware colander.* **LEFT** *Briny mussels catch the carrots and shallots that thicken the herbed liquid I created for baby artichokes.*

ABOVE *Delicate strands of spaghetti squash are dressed in a tangy vinaigrette with whole sage leaves.* OPPOSITE *No healthy kitchen is complete without parchment paper, which has a multitude of culinary uses, from baking en papillote (in paper), as I do here, to making pastry bags to lining baking sheets.*

Spaghetti Squash with Sage and Orange

1   2¹/₂-pound spaghetti squash, halved lengthwise, seeds removed, and quartered lengthwise

1   small orange, finely zested and juiced (about 1¹/₂ teaspoons zest and 3 teaspoons juice)

¹/₂   teaspoon Dijon mustard

1¹/₂   teaspoons extra-virgin olive oil

2   teaspoons coarsely chopped fresh sage leaves, plus 3 whole leaves for garnish

Kosher salt and freshly ground black pepper

SERVES 4

In a large saucepan filled with a steamer rack placed at least 1 inch above the boiling water, place the squash flesh side down. Cover and steam until the squash is fork-tender but not mushy, about 15 minutes. Cool the squash slightly. To release the spaghetti strands, drag a fork from end to end as you would a rake and place in a serving bowl. In a small bowl, whisk together the orange zest, juice, mustard, olive oil, sage, and salt and pepper. Toss with the squash and garnish with the sage leaves.

Forelle Pears in Parchment

2   Forelle pears, halved and cored

2   cinnamon sticks, halved lengthwise

1   vanilla bean, halved lengthwise, then widthwise

8   ¹/₂-inch-long strips candied ginger

¹/₄   cup golden raisins

2   tablespoons dark raisins

1   lemon, zested into strips with a vegetable peeler and minced

¹/₂   cup port wine

1   teaspoon unsalted butter

SERVES 4

Preheat the oven to 350°F. Fold four 12 × 18-inch sheets of parchment paper in half and cut to make 4 heart shapes about 5 inches larger in circumference than the pear half. Place a pear half near the fold and place a piece of cinnamon stick, vanilla bean, 2 pieces of ginger, one quarter of each of the raisins, and one quarter of the lemon zest on top of the pear. Drizzle with 2 tablespoons wine. Divide the butter into fourths and dot the tops of each pear.

Fold the paper to enclose the pear and make small overlapping folds to seal the edges, starting at the curve of the heart. Be sure each fold overlaps the one before it so that there are no gaps. Repeat with the remaining pears.

Place the packages on a baking sheet and bake for 40 minutes. The parchment will be golden brown and the pears will yield when pricked with a fork. Score the parchment in an X shape, peel it back, and serve.

MENU · POSOLE WITH GARNISHES · WARM CORN TORTILLAS · CARAMELIZED PLANTAINS · SERVES 4

The perfect informal supper, posole, a traditional Mexican main-course soup, is a beautiful and wonderfully satisfying one-pot meal. When I have the time or can plan ahead, I use dried hominy. It requires pre-soaking overnight or boiling, then simmering for 1 hour. Canned hominy is often a more realistic choice given my busy schedule, and is available in supermarkets, natural foods stores, and specialty markets. Once you've made these corn tortillas, you'll never settle for the dried-out, bland commercial varieties. While you can make tortillas without a tortilla press, or comal, I strongly recommend using one. They are inexpensive and widely available at specialty kitchen stores. Alternatively, press the dough between two flat plates. If you can't find plantains, bananas are just as delicious.

Posole with Garnishes

1	teaspoon extra-virgin olive oil
1	medium-size yellow onion, diced (about 1½ cups)
2	medium-size garlic cloves
1½	teaspoons cumin
1	teaspoon kosher salt
1	16-ounce can hominy, drained
1	small jalapeño pepper
1	pound tomatillos, diced (about 3 cups)
2	bunches Swiss chard, coarsely chopped (about 26 ounces)
4	cups Chicken Stock (page 13) or low-sodium canned
2	bay leaves

GARNISHES

8	radishes, very thinly sliced
2	jalapeño peppers, very thinly sliced
1	small avocado, peeled, halved, pitted, and quartered
8	scallions, very thinly sliced
2	tablespoons sour cream
2	limes, quartered
	Chile de arbol powder
8	sprigs of fresh cilantro, coarsely chopped

SERVES 4

Heat the oil in a large pot. Add the onion and garlic, cover, and cook, stirring occasionally, until the onion is soft, about 5 minutes. Add the cumin and salt and cook until fragrant, about 30 seconds. Add the hominy, jalapeño, and tomatillos and cook, stirring, for 1 minute. Add the Swiss chard, stock, and bay leaves and bring to a boil. Cover and cook, stirring, until the chard is wilted and the leaves are tender, about 20 minutes. Remove the bay leaf.

Ladle the soup into 4 bowls and garnish each serving with radishes, jalapeños, avocado, scallions, sour cream, and 2 lime wedges. Sprinkle with chile de arbol powder and top with the chopped cilantro sprigs.

RIGHT *I like to set out the Posole with Garnishes buffet style. Yellow stoneware and a sturdy lidded stone serving bowl sit on an antique milk glass table.*

ABOVE *Plantains aren't meant for eating right out of the peel, but they are transformed into a gently sweet dessert when caramelized.* **OPPOSITE** *Masa harina, water, and a tortilla press are all you need to make fresh, uniformly thin corn tortillas.*

Warm Corn Tortillas

1	cup masa harina
½–¾	cup boiling water

MAKES 4 TORTILLAS

In a small bowl, combine the masa harina and water, then knead until smooth, adding more water if necessary to achieve a soft, claylike consistency.

Prepare 5 pieces of parchment the size of your tortilla press. Place one piece on the bottom of the press. Place a ball of dough about the size of a walnut on the parchment. Cover with a piece of parchment, close the top plate, and press down firmly with the handle. Rotate the tortilla and press again, if necessary, to flatten the tortilla to a ¹⁄₁₆-inch thickness. Open the press, peel the top piece of parchment off the tortilla and reuse for remaining dough. Repeat with the remaining dough. Stack the tortillas on top of one another and cover the stack with a damp kitchen towel.

Heat a dry cast-iron skillet or nonstick pan until moderately hot. Hold one tortilla in your hand, peel the parchment away, lay the tortilla in the skillet, and cook 30 to 45 seconds per side. Repeat with the remaining tortillas, stacking them as you go. Serve immediately.

Caramelized Plantains

1	tablespoon unsalted butter
1	tablespoon sugar
2	plantains (sweet), cut into ⅓-inch slices
⅓	cup apple juice
1½	teaspoons ground cinnamon

SERVES 4

In a 9-inch skillet, melt the butter over medium heat. Add the sugar and cook, stirring, until the syrup is a light caramel color, about 2 minutes. Add the plantains, tossing to coat, and cook until tender, about 3 minutes. Add the apple juice and boil 1 minute, or until thickened slightly. Stir in the cinnamon and remove from the heat. Divide the plantains among 4 dessert plates and spoon the juices over each.

MENU · GRILLED ARTICHOKES WITH
RAW TOMATO COMPOTE · WILD MUSHROOM SOUP ·
STRAWBERRIES IN SWEET VANILLA SYRUP · SERVES 4

It is no secret that eating a variety of foods is the key to maintaining good eating habits. But it is only part of the equation. A mix of textures and colors prevents boredom and repetition, and sitting down to an exquisitely presented meal, no matter how simple the ingredients, is both physically and emotionally satisfying. This menu features a host of flavors, textures, temperatures, and colors. The compote is best served cold with the grilled artichokes, but is equally good just heated through and spooned over steamed fish or grilled bread. Use the broth for the Wild Mushroom Soup as a blueprint for making all manner of stocks—simply combine the discarded ends of vegetables with water and herbs and simmer, skimming the broth occasionally. Freeze them in tightly covered containers and use as needed. As much as I love a bowl of just-picked strawberries for dessert, I will often toss them in a simple vanilla syrup sweetened with fruit juice and a little sugar, a wonderful, quick way to make any fresh berries special.

Grilled Artichokes with Raw Tomato Compote

4   *large artichokes (about 2¼ pounds)*
2   *lemons, halved*
2   *teaspoons extra-virgin olive oil*
    Raw Tomato Compote (recipe follows)

SERVES 4

Prepare a stove-top griddle or outdoor grill.

Snap off the tough outer leaves of the artichokes and discard. Rub the exposed surfaces with a lemon half. Cut off about the top third of each artichoke with a sharp knife. Trim the ends of the leaves with scissors. Trim all but ½ inch of the stem. Using a stainless-steel knife or a curved "bird's beak" knife, pare the remaining stem. Steam the artichokes for 20 minutes. When cool, halve each and, using a melon baller, scoop out the prickly hairs, or the choke, and keep scraping until no more fuzz is apparent. Brush the halves with olive oil. Grill each side for 5 to 7 minutes, until the artichokes are nicely browned. Spoon the tomato compote into each half and serve.

Raw Tomato Compote

1   *garlic clove, finely chopped*
2   *scallions, white part only, finely chopped*
2   *teaspoons extra-virgin olive oil*
6   *plum tomatoes, seeded and coarsely chopped*
½   *cup coarsely chopped basil leaves*
2   *teaspoons sugar*
¼   *cup good-quality wine vinegar*
     Kosher salt and freshly ground black pepper

MAKES 1½ CUPS

Combine all of the ingredients in a medium bowl and toss. Season to taste with salt and pepper. The compote will keep, tightly covered, in the refrigerator for 2 days.

OPPOSITE AND ABOVE *Nothing symbolizes spring more perfectly than artichokes.*

41

Wild Mushroom Soup

FOR THE BROTH

	Reserved mushroom stems
2	medium carrots, halved crosswise
1	bay leaf
5	peppercorns
4	sprigs of fresh thyme

FOR THE SOUP

1	pound assorted wild mushrooms (oysters, shiitakes, chanterelles, horn of plenty, porcini), cleaned and trimmed, stem ends reserved
1	red onion, ½ peeled and very thinly sliced, ½ coarsely chopped
	Kosher salt and freshly ground black pepper

SERVES 4

Combine the broth ingredients with 2 quarts of cold water and bring to a boil. Reduce the heat to low and simmer 20 to 30 minutes. Meanwhile, slice the mushrooms into ¼-inch strips. Strain the broth. Add the onion to the broth and cook over low heat 3 to 5 minutes. Add the mushrooms and cook until they are tender, about 35 minutes. Season to taste with salt and pepper. Ladle into shallow soup bowls and garnish with the thyme.

Strawberries and Vanilla Syrup

1	cup white grape juice
1	tablespoon lemon juice
¼	cup sugar
1	vanilla bean
1	pint fresh strawberries, washed, hulled, and sliced
	Mint leaves, for garnish

SERVES 4

In a small saucepan, combine the juices, sugar, and vanilla bean and bring to a boil. Reduce the heat and simmer 15 minutes, or until the liquid is reduced by half. Stir in the strawberries, remove from the heat, and divide among 4 dessert goblets. Garnish with mint leaves and serve.

OPPOSITE *I used to have to make a special trip to find the exquisite variety of wild mushrooms featured in this soup. Now, virtually any large supermarket offers a good selection.* **BELOW** *Rather than serving these beautiful strawberries in a traditional dessert dish, I love using simple blown-glass tumblers.*

MENU · COLD TOFU SALAD WITH SOY GINGER DIPPING SAUCE · VEGETABLE HANDROLLS · GINGER ICE MILK · SERVES 4

I have long been drawn to the simple, clean flavors of and aesthetic genius of Japanese food. Now that supermarkets all over the country carry once exotic ingredients such as nori (seaweed paper), I can prepare simple versions of the dishes that initially lured me to explore this inherently healthful cuisine. I love tofu prepared as it is here, sliced super thin, infused with soothing fresh ginger, and eaten with chopsticks. Serve the handrolls with individual dipping sauce bowls filled with the soy sauce and a pinch of wasabi. Each person can stir the wasabi paste into the soy sauce as desired. Pickled ginger preserved in sweet vinegar is traditionally eaten throughout the meal and should be presented in a tiny pile on each plate. If you have never had Ginger Ice Milk, it will be a revelation! When I crave the flavor but don't have the time to make this version, I stir pieces of minced candied ginger into softened vanilla ice milk.

Cold Tofu Salad with Soy Ginger Dipping Sauce

2   cups cracked ice
¹/2   pound firm tofu, drained and cut into
        ¹/4-inch strips
4   scallions, white part only, thinly sliced
2   teaspoons black sesame seeds
¹/4   cup Soy Ginger Dipping Sauce (recipe
        follows)
1   cherry tomato, cut into 4 wedges for
        garnish

    SERVES 4

Fill 4 small salad bowls with cracked ice. Arrange the tofu on top of the ice, and top with some scallions and sesame seeds. Drizzle with the dipping sauce, garnish with the tomato, and serve.

Soy Ginger Dipping Sauce

¹/2 · cup low-sodium soy sauce
3   tablespoons rice vinegar
1   teaspoon peeled and finely minced
        fresh ginger
1   scallion, thinly sliced for garnish

    MAKES ³/4 CUP

In a small bowl, combine the soy sauce, vinegar, and ginger. Garnish with the scallion and serve.

LEFT *Distinctly flavored ingredients, including nori sheets, sushi rice, beautifully sliced vegetables, pickled ginger, fiery wasabi, soy sauce, and mirin wine, combine to form the sublime Vegetable Handrolls.* RIGHT *Cold Tofu Salad with Soy Ginger Dipping Sauce is elegant, pure, and deceptively simple to prepare.*

Vegetable Handrolls

8	7 × 4-inch nori sheets
2	tablespoons mirin wine
1	cup Sushi Rice (page 195)
8	thin asparagus
8	4-inch-long daikon slices, julienned
8	4-inch-long peeled cucumber slices, julienned
8	scallion greens
1	tablespoon prepared wasabi paste
½	cup low-sodium soy sauce
¼	cup pickled ginger

MAKES 8 ROLLS

Brush the rough matte side of a sheet of nori with the wine. Place the sheet on the counter and spoon the rice in a 1-inch-wide strip across the middle of the sheet. Place one of each vegetable on top. Roll the nori as in a waffle cone by grasping the upper right corner of the nori between your thumb and middle finger and folding it over the rice to meet the opposite side. Pick up the lower left corner and wrap it around to form a cone. Serve with the wasabi, soy sauce, and pickled ginger.

Ginger Ice Milk

3½	cups low-fat milk
½	cup sugar
1	3-inch piece of fresh ginger, peeled and thinly sliced
1	teaspoon ground ginger
⅛	teaspoon kosher salt
	Candied ginger, for garnish (optional)

MAKES 1 QUART

Combine the milk and sugar in a 2-quart saucepan over medium heat. Heat, stirring occasionally, until the sugar has dissolved and the mixture is hot. Add the fresh ginger and reduce the heat to low. Heat, barely simmering, for 15 minutes. Remove from the heat and add the ground ginger. Set aside to infuse for at least 45 minutes, or until the ginger flavor suits your taste. (Remember that the flavor will not be as strong when the mixture is frozen.) Remove the pieces of ginger, add the salt, cover, and chill thoroughly.

Freeze in an ice cream maker according to the manufacturer's directions. Garnish each serving with a few strips of candied ginger, if desired.

BELOW *Slightly sweet, somewhat peppery, and totally refreshing, Ginger Ice Milk is infused with fresh, powdered, and candied ginger.* **OPPOSITE** *Stir a bit of the wasabi paste into the soy sauce, pick up the nori-wrapped roll with your hands, and dip it into the mixture after each bite, adding more wasabi as you go. Eat the pickled ginger with your fingers, too.*

MENU · HOT AND SOUR BROTH WITH SHREDDED CHICKEN · GINGERED STICKY RICE · ICED LYCHEES · SERVES 4

Hot and Sour Broth is my version of the classic Chinese hot and sour soup. Unlike the traditional version, this broth is very light. If you cannot find the mushrooms or other ingredients, improvise. Gingered Sticky Rice is simple to make. I like to spoon some into the broth to create a sturdy yet light meal in a bowl. Juicy and sweet lychees are available in late spring. Best eaten right out of their pockmarked blush-red skins, the creamy white flesh is quite refreshing.

Hot and Sour Broth with Shredded Chicken

6   large dried black mushrooms, lightly washed
6   dried tree ear mushrooms, lightly washed
6   dried tiger lily buds
4–8 fresh thai chili peppers, or to taste
6   cups Chicken Stock (page 13) or low-sodium canned or water
1   chicken breast, poached and shredded
½   cup thinly sliced bamboo or bamboo shoots
2   medium carrots, cut into matchsticks
½   pound firm tofu, cut into ½-inch cubes
¼   cup chopped scallions
¼   cup cilantro leaves
1   lime, zested

SERVES 4

In a large saucepan or stockpot, combine the black and tree ear mushrooms, tiger lily buds, and chili peppers with the stock or water. Bring to a boil. Remove from the heat and steep for 30 minutes. Remove 2 black and 4 tree ear mushrooms, cut into ¼-inch slices, and reserve. Reheat the stock until almost boiling. Divide the chicken, bamboo, carrots, tofu, and scallions among 4 bowls. Pour the hot broth into the bowls and garnish with the reserved mushrooms, cilantro leaves, and lime, and serve.

Gingered Sticky Rice

½   cup short-grain rice
5   quarter-sized slices fresh ginger
    Pinch of kosher salt

MAKES 2 CUPS; SERVES 4

Combine all of the ingredients with 1¼ cups of water in a saucepan and cook over moderately low heat, covered, for 20 minutes, until the rice is tender. Remove the ginger slices and serve.

Iced Lychees

3   cups shaved ice
¾   cup grapefruit juice
2   pounds lychees, partially peeled

SERVES 4

Spread the ice evenly on a serving tray (preferably one of clear glass). Pour the grapefruit juice over the ice. Arrange the lychees over the ice and serve. To eat, peel the rough skin away from the fruit, enjoy the juicy flesh, and discard the pit.

LEFT *I always serve fresh lychees partially peeled and sitting atop crushed ice drenched in pink grapefruit juice.* RIGHT *Cradle a bowl of fragrant Hot and Sour Broth in your hands and sip the broth right from the rim.*

MENU · GOLDEN BRUSCHETTA ·
POACHED SALMON TROUT WITH POPPY SEED VINAIGRETTE ·
RICOTTA WITH GROUND ESPRESSO · SERVES 4

Salmon trout, named for its pretty pink hue, looks similar to coho salmon, but it is not salmon at all; it is a brown trout that swims from lakes and streams to the sea, and is sometimes referred to as steelhead. Brook trout and rainbow trout are also good poached, a technique that is restrained enough to preserve the delicate flavor of any of these fish. Bruschetta is typically served as an appetizer or midday snack, but for this menu, I prefer to eat it along with my fish. Sometimes I simplify the bruschetta even more by grilling, drizzling very good quality olive oil and lightly salting the bread. For dessert, low-fat ricotta sweetened with honey is surprisingly rich and decadent—and won't leave you feeling uncomfortably full.

Golden Bruschetta

4   ¼-inch-thick slices brioche
½   pound pear tomatoes, halved
½   cup assorted fresh herbs (basil, tarragon, thyme, dill, chives)
2   teaspoons extra-virgin olive oil
    Kosher salt and freshly ground black pepper

SERVES 4

Grill or toast the bread slices until golden and crisp. Set aside. In a small bowl, toss together the tomatoes, herbs, olive oil, and salt and pepper. Spoon a quarter of the mixture onto each brioche slice, season with additional pepper, and serve.

Poached Salmon Trout with Poppy Seed Vinaigrette

2   cups white wine
1   teaspoon whole black peppercorns
1   bay leaf
4   medium leeks, white part only, halved lengthwise, or 4 whole baby leeks
1   16-ounce salmon trout or coho salmon, gutted, head and tail removed
2   tablespoons Poppy Seed Vinaigrette (page 17)
    Lemon wedges, for garnish

SERVES 4

In a poacher or large roasting pan, combine the wine, peppercorns, and bay leaf with 1 cup of water. Bring to a boil, then reduce to a simmer. There should be about 1 to 1½ inches of liquid in the pan.

Add the leeks and arrange the fish on top. Cover and simmer until the leeks are tender and the fish is opaque, 12 to 18 minutes.

Arrange the fish and leeks on a platter. Add salt and pepper and drizzle the vinaigrette on top. Garnish with lemon wedges and serve.

Ricotta with Ground Espresso

1   15-ounce container part-skim ricotta
¼   cup honey
¼   cup strong espresso, chilled
1   tablespoon espresso beans, ground

SERVES 4

In a mixing bowl, beat together the ricotta and honey until light and smooth, about 5 minutes. Spoon evenly among 4 dessert dishes, drizzle 1 tablespoon of espresso into each dish, and sprinkle the ground espresso beans on top.

RIGHT *Spoon herb-spiked pear tomatoes onto paper-thin slices of grilled brioche.* OVERLEAF, LEFT *Poached salmon trout and leeks are arranged on an oval pewter platter with steel-bladed, bone-handled cutlery.* OVERLEAF, RIGHT *Part-skim ricotta drizzled with a bit of espresso and crowned with fine-ground espresso beans is an easy elegant dessert.*

MENU · BEEF BARLEY SOUP · ROASTED BEET SALAD ·
PINEAPPLE UPSIDE-DOWN CAKES · SERVES 4

Beef Barley Soup

1	tablespoon extra-virgin olive oil
1/2	pound stew beef, cut into 1/2-inch pieces
1	medium-size yellow onion, coarsely chopped
2	medium carrots, cut into 1/4-inch coins
1	medium garlic clove, finely minced
6	cups Beef Stock (page 14) or low-sodium canned
1/4	cup barley, rinsed
2	teaspoons coarsely chopped fresh thyme
	Parsley, for garnish

SERVES 4

All you need to add to this menu to make a satisfying meal is a hearty piece of rustic country bread. Toasted caraway seeds infuse the Roasted Beet Salad with subtle hints of anise and lemon. Dry-toasting seeds and spices releases their flavor, giving most any dish incredible depth without adding a bit of fat. Prepare the salad and best-ever version of classic beef barley soup first, and while they're cooking mix the ingredients for the slimmed-down version of traditional pineapple upside-down cake. Slide the cakes in the oven when you sit down to eat and they'll be ready just in time for dessert.

In a 6-quart soup pot, heat 2 teaspoons of the olive oil over medium-high heat. Add the meat and brown evenly, about 5 minutes. Using a slotted spoon, transfer the meat to a paper towel–lined plate. Reduce the heat to medium. Add the remaining oil and the onion and cook until the onion is soft and translucent, about 10 minutes, scraping the pot to loosen any brown bits. Add the carrots and garlic and sweat 5 minutes, stirring occasionally. Add 1/2 cup of stock and scrape the bottom of the pot. Add the remaining stock, the meat, barley, and thyme and bring to a boil. Reduce the heat and simmer, skimming the pot occasionally, until the barley is cooked and the meat is tender, about 50 minutes. Ladle into deep bowls and serve, garnished with parsley.

Roasted Beet Salad

8	small beets, cleaned and trimmed (about 2 pounds)
2	teaspoons caraway seeds
2	tablespoons extra-virgin olive oil
2	tablespoons balsamic vinegar
	Kosher salt and freshly ground black pepper
2	cups red oak leaf lettuce

SERVES 4

Preheat the oven to 425°F.

Wrap the beets in parchment paper, place on a small baking sheet, and roast in the oven until they yield to a paring knife, about 35 to 50 minutes.

Meanwhile, in a dry skillet over medium-low heat, toast the caraway seeds until fragrant, about 1 minute. Whisk together the oil and vinegar, add the toasted caraway seeds, and season with salt and pepper. Set aside.

When the beets have cooled, peel and cut them into eighths. Toss the beets in the dressing. Divide the lettuce among 4 salad plates and arrange the beets on top.

OPPOSITE *Ruby-red beets show their true color when served on my Lu-ray lunch plates.*

Pineapple Upside-Down Cakes

¼   cup sugar, plus 1 teaspoon for
       sprinkling
4   ¼-inch-thick slices fresh pineapple,
       peeled and cored
½   cup sifted cake flour
½   teaspoon baking powder
       Pinch of kosher salt
2   tablespoons vegetable oil
3   tablespoons frozen pineapple juice
       concentrate, at room temperature
¼   teaspoon pure vanilla extract
2   large egg whites
1   tablespoon sifted confectioners' sugar

SERVES 4

Place a rack in the center of the oven and preheat to 350°F.

Spray four 4-inch-wide shallow ramekins with nonstick cooking spray. Sprinkle the bottom of each with ¼ teaspoon sugar, place a slice of pineapple in each ramekin, and set aside.

Sift together the flour, remaining sugar, baking powder, and salt into a large mixing bowl. Make a well in the center of the dry ingredients and add the olive oil, pineapple juice concentrate, and vanilla. Set aside.

In another large mixing bowl, beat the egg whites until they are white and foamy, about 1 minute. Add the confectioners' sugar and continue beating until stiff but not dry, about 2 minutes. Scrape off the beaters and,

without washing them, place in the flour mixture and beat at low speed just until blended. Gently fold the flour mixture into the egg whites. Pour one quarter of the batter into each ramekin and bake for 25 minutes, or until a cake tester inserted in the center comes out clean.

Cool the cakes on a wire rack. With a sharp knife, loosen the sides of the cakes. Invert onto the rack, lift off the ramekins, and cool. Serve warm.

ABOVE *I love eating chunky soup out of bowls like this contemporary hand-thrown porcelain soup bowl. The generous proportions of the fiddlehead flatware is perfect for scooping up every bit of soup.* **RIGHT** *Once cooled, individual Pineapple Upside-Down Cakes can be immediately turned out onto dessert plates. These are part of my jadeite collection.*

MENU · CORN, FAVA BEAN, AND CUCUMBER SUCCOTASH · ASSORTED STEAMED CLAMS · SKILLET FLATBREAD · FROZEN LEMONADE · SERVES 4

The transition from spring to summer is always bittersweet. Young fava beans, tender fiddleheads, and garlicky ramps give over their space in the market to garden-fresh tomatoes, corn, and cucumbers. During that very short time when the bounty of both seasons is available, I take full advantage. Choose small, crisp fava beans for the succotash and use whatever herbs are the freshest in the flatbread. Make the dough for the flatbread first, then prepare the succotash. Steam the clams last and serve them hot with individual bowls of broth for rinsing.

Corn, Fava Bean, and Cucumber Succotash

1	cup fresh fava beans (from about 20 pods)
2	teaspoons canola oil
2	tablespoons finely diced white onion
1	English cucumber, peeled, seeded, and coarsely chopped
	Kosher salt and freshly ground black pepper
1	cup fresh corn kernels (from about 2 ears)
½	cup diced red bell pepper
2	teaspoons chopped fresh tarragon

SERVES 4

Blanch the fava beans in boiling water for 3 minutes. Drain well. When the beans are cool enough to handle, remove their skins. Set the beans aside.

Heat the canola oil in a large skillet over low heat. Add the onion and cook until transparent but not brown, about 5 minutes.

Raise the heat to medium and add the cucumber. Season lightly with salt and pepper. Cook until the cucumber is tender, about 6 minutes. If the onion begins to brown, add a tablespoon or two of water and continue cooking.

Add the corn and cook 1 to 2 minutes. Add the fava beans and bell pepper. Season and cook 2 minutes more, until tender. Stir in the tarragon and serve.

Assorted Steamed Clams

1	cup dry white wine
2	tablespoons Pernod
1	medium-size onion, thinly sliced
3	garlic cloves, peeled and smashed
½	cup assorted fresh herbs (thyme, rosemary, tarragon)
3	dozen assorted clams (littleneck, Manila, steamer, razor, or yellow)
12	sprigs of parsley

SERVES 4

Combine the wine, Pernod, onion, and garlic in a large pot with a tight-fitting lid. Bring to a boil, then reduce to a simmer and cook for 3 or 4 minutes. Add the herbs. Add the clams and cook, shaking the pot several times, until the clams open, 3 or 4 minutes. Discard any clams that do not open.

Spoon the clams into shallow soup bowls, spoon in some of the broth, and garnish with the parsley. Serve immediately.

LEFT *A dash of Pernod added to the steaming liquid infuses tender, juicy clams with a subtle hint of licorice flavor.* RIGHT *Canola oil and tarragon flavors the very freshest young corn, small fava beans, and sweet red bell peppers.*

Skillet Flatbread

1   *cup plus 3 tablespoons all-purpose flour*
¹/₂   *teaspoon baking powder*
1   *teaspoon kosher salt*
2   *teaspoons finely chopped chives*
2¹/₂ *tablespoons vegetable shortening*
3   *tablespoons milk*
1   *tablespoon extra-virgin olive oil*

MAKES 3 6¹/₂-INCH-WIDE ROUNDS;
SERVES 4

In the bowl of a food processor, combine the flour, baking powder, ¹/₂ teaspoon salt, and chives and process for 5 seconds to combine. Add the shortening and process until well combined, about 15 seconds. Add the milk and 2 tablespoons water. Process to bring the dough together. Remove from the processor and knead 1 minute to form a ball. Cover with plastic wrap and set aside for 30 minutes.

Heat a cast-iron skillet until very hot. Divide the dough into 3 pieces and form each into a ball. On a lightly floured surface, roll out the dough in a 6¹/₂-inch-diameter circle to less than ¹/₁₆ inch thick. Prick the dough with a fork, brush with the olive oil, and sprinkle with the kosher salt. Transfer the round of dough, with the oiled side down, to the hot skillet and reduce the heat to medium. Cook about 1 to 2 minutes on each side, until the surface is covered with golden to dark brown speckles. Remove the bread from the skillet and transfer to a baking sheet in a warm oven. Repeat the rolling and cooking process with the remaining dough. Cut the bread into wedges with a pizza wheel or sharp knife and serve.

Frozen Lemonade

4   *lemons, juiced*
1   *orange, juiced*
1   *lemongrass stalk, chopped into 1-inch pieces*
¹/₂   *cup sugar*
1   *tablespoon honey*

MAKES 1 QUART

In a medium bowl, combine the lemon and orange juices with the lemongrass and set aside for 30 minutes or overnight in the refrigerator. Add 4 cups of water, the sugar, and honey. Pour into a baking pan and freeze 1 to 2 hours. Using a fork, loosen the lemonade from the pan and return to the freezer for 20 minutes more. Scoop into the chilled bowl of a food processor and purée until smooth. Spoon among 4 tall glasses and serve.

ABOVE *Fresh herbs mixed into the dough give Skillet Flatbread a distinctly spring hue.* **RIGHT** *Scoops of tangy Frozen Lemonade are stacked in etched-glass Depression tumblers.*

MENU · SPRING LINGUINE ·
SAUTÉED MORELS · LIME SOUFFLÉ · SERVES 4

As soon as the air warms and sun shines later into the day, I set a table in my garden. I love using casual linens like this runner fashioned from kitchen toweling, which is often sold off the bolt in specialty fabric stores. This menu features some of my favorite, if somewhat unusual, spring ingredients. Fiddleheads are edible ferns that grow wild along the fertile banks of rivers and streams. You may find them with a rather unattractive brown, somewhat papery residue on them, which should simply be washed off before preparing them. Morels, edible wild mushrooms that are prized for their smoky, nutty flavor, will also need thorough washing, since they are riddled with nooks and crannies. I prefer the wild variety, usually available from April through June. Cultivated morels, on the other hand, are available throughout the year. I serve the morels as a side dish here, but they just as easily could be tossed into the pasta. For dessert, featherweight, luscious Lime Soufflé is deceptively simple—and very quick—to make.

Spring Linguine

1	pound linguine
½	pound fiddleheads
	Kosher salt and freshly ground black pepper
1	teaspoon lemon juice
2	tablespoons olive oil
½	pound baby leeks, washed, trimmed, and cut into thirds on a bias
1½	cups dandelion greens or sorrel, washed

SERVES 4

In a large pot of boiling, salted water, cook the linguine until al dente. Drain and transfer to a large bowl.

Meanwhile, remove the papery particles from the fiddleheads. Fill a medium bowl with cool water; add 1 teaspoon salt and the lemon juice. Add the fiddleheads, and push them down into the water several times to clean them. Transfer them to a steamer rack in a saucepan and steam, covered, about 4 to 5 minutes.

Heat the olive oil in a large skillet over medium heat. Add the leeks and sauté for 2 to 3 minutes, until soft. Add the fiddleheads and cook 1 to 2 minutes more, until warm and golden. Stir in the dandelion greens. Toss the mixture with the pasta, season with salt and pepper, and serve.

Sauteed Morels

1	tablespoon butter
1	garlic clove, minced
¼	to ½ pound morels
¼	cup Chicken Stock (page 13) or low-sodium canned
1	tablespoon white wine
	Kosher salt and freshly ground black pepper

SERVES 4

Melt the butter in a large pan over medium heat. Add the garlic and cook until soft and golden. Add the morels and cook, stirring, until they begin to exude their juices, about 2 to 3 minutes. Add the stock and wine and cook 2 minutes more until heated through. Season with salt and pepper and serve.

ABOVE *Named for their resemblance to the spiral end of a fiddle, fiddleheads unfurl into beautiful ferns two weeks after their tightly coiled shoots appear.* **OPPOSITE** *The Sautéed Morels are an ideal accompaniment to linguine studded with baby leeks and chewy fiddleheads and finished with a squeeze of lemon juice.*

BELOW *Morels taste best unadorned; I usually sauté them in a little butter and finish them with a dash of white wine. Serve them on a bed of fresh flowering chives.* **OPPOSITE** *Simple, sublime, and virtually fat-free, the billowy Lime Soufflé calls for just six ingredients.*

Lime Soufflé

	Granulated sugar
½	*cup superfine sugar*
¼	*cup fresh lime juice*
4	*egg whites, at room temperature*
¼	*teaspoon kosher salt*
2	*teaspoons grated lime zest*

SERVES 4

Preheat the oven to 400°F. Spray a 1-quart soufflé dish with nonstick cooking spray and dust generously with granulated sugar. Place the soufflé dish in the freezer to chill.

Stir ¼ cup of the superfine sugar with the lime juice in a small bowl until the sugar is dissolved. Set aside. Using very clean, dry beaters, beat the egg whites by hand or with an electric mixer until foamy. Gradually add the remaining ¼ cup of superfine sugar and the salt while beating. Continue beating until the whites hold a soft peak. Gently fold in the lime juice mixture and the zest.

Spoon the soufflé mixture into the chilled soufflé dish. Wipe the rim with your fingers or a damp cloth to ensure proper rising. Put the dish on a baking sheet and place in the oven immediately. Bake for 7 to 9 minutes, until the soufflé is well risen and lightly browned on top. Serve and eat immediately.

MENU · WINE-POACHED CHICKEN WITH CHARMOULA · CHOPPED SALAD WITH TARRAGON VINAIGRETTE · MOROCCAN PUDDING · SERVES 4

Charmoula is a spicy Moroccan marinade that typically contains paprika, cumin, and garlic. The turmeric turns the couscous the color of the brilliant summer sun and I like to spread it on a plate in a sunburst. Succulent romaine is the perfect green to serve with this pungent chicken dish; the midribs are particularly cool and refreshing. For dessert, Moroccan Pudding is tapioca with a North African twist.

Wine-Poached Chicken with Charmoula

2	cups dry white wine
4	whole sprigs of fresh cilantro
6	whole black peppercorns
2	8-ounce whole chicken breasts
	Kosher salt and freshly ground black pepper

COUSCOUS

1½	cups Chicken Stock (page 13) or low-sodium canned, fat skimmed
1	cup couscous
½	teaspoon turmeric

CHARMOULA

1	tablespoon ground cumin
1	teaspoon paprika
½	teaspoon cayenne pepper
1	tablespooon minced garlic
3	tablespoons fresh lemon juice
2	teaspoons extra-virgin olive oil
⅓	cup finely chopped flat-leaf parsley
⅓	cup tomato juice
⅓	cup chopped fresh cilantro leaves
½	teaspoon kosher salt
⅛	teaspoon freshly ground pepper

SERVES 4

In a high-sided frying pan or braiser, combine the wine, cilantro, and peppercorns. Bring to a boil, reduce the heat, and simmer. Add the chicken and poach, turning once, about 12 to 15 minutes. Season to taste with salt and pepper. Remove to a cutting board to rest.

Meanwhile, bring the stock to a boil. Add the couscous, stir, and bring to a second boil. Remove from the heat, cover, and let stand 5 minutes. Stir in the turmeric.

Combine the charmoula ingredients in a small bowl. Cut the chicken breasts in half. Divide the couscous among 4 dinner plates and arrange chicken breasts on top. Serve each with ¼ cup of the charmoula.

LEFT *Lemon, garlic, herbs, and spices are combined to create a wonderful sauce for chicken and shrimp.* RIGHT *Humble ingredients tossed in tangy tarragon vinaigrette and piled high on a salad plate make a delicious salad.*

ABOVE *Tapioca pudding, Moroccan-style: simmered golden apricots and raisins spiked with cinnamon and ginger are spooned over smooth, creamy tapioca.* **OPPOSITE** *Poached chicken is the perfect canvas for ultra-spicy charmoula sauce.*

Chopped Salad with Tarragon Vinaigrette

1   *red onion, diced*
2   *medium-size tomatoes, diced*
½   *hothouse cucumber, halved lengthwise and diced*
¼   *cup pitted Kalamata olives, quartered*
1   *large head romaine lettuce, leaves stacked and sliced into ¼-inch strips, strips halved crosswise*
½   *cup Tarragon Vinaigrette (page 16)*

SERVES 4

In a large bowl, combine all of the ingredients and toss with your hands until evenly distributed. To serve, gather a handful of salad and gently drop it onto a salad plate, forming a pyramid.

Moroccan Pudding

1   *large egg, separated*
¼   *cup plus ½ teaspoon sugar*
2   *tablespoons instant tapioca*
1½   *cups lowfat (1%) milk*
½   *teaspoon pure vanilla extract*
½   *tablespoon unsalted butter*
4   *fresh apricots, pitted and quartered*
1   *tablespoon milk*
2   *tablespoons golden raisins*
¼   *teaspoon cinnamon*
¼   *teaspoon ground ginger*

SERVES 4

In a small bowl, beat the egg white with an electric mixer until foamy. Gradually add 2 tablespoons sugar, beating until soft peaks form, and reserve.

In a saucepan, whisk together 2 tablespoons of sugar, the tapioca, milk, vanilla, and egg yolk. Let stand 5 minutes. Cook the mixture over moderate heat, stirring constantly, until it comes to a full boil. Remove the pan from the heat and immediately stir in the reserved egg white. Return the mixture to low heat and cook, stirring constantly, for 2 minutes. Cool the tapioca, its surface covered in plastic wrap, for 20 minutes.

In a nonstick skillet, melt the butter. Add the apricots and the remaining ½ teaspoon sugar and cook over moderate heat, stirring occasionally, for 2 to 3 minutes. Add the tablespoon of milk and stir to coat. Remove from the heat and stir in the raisins, cinnamon, and ginger. Divide the tapioca among 4 bowls and top with the apricot mixture.

SUMMER

Healthy cooking and eating are synonymous with summer. I try to spend my weekends in and around the garden at this time of year—weeding, replanting, and picking the fruits of my labor. Menus that rely on the delicate flavors of Mother Nature's springtime now become more robust with the abundance of the summer garden. What the garden doesn't provide, the farmstands do. It is a pleasure to cook on the eastern end of Long Island, where I try to go each weekend, because the raw ingredients are so available—sweet, dense, deep red, and mineralized strawberries, seriously tasty celery, mixtures of greens that actually taste of individual flavors, and herbs and young root vegetables that have true color and intensity of flavor. Another thing that makes the summertime table so very delightful is the prevalence of fresh seafood—small, tender lobsters, tiny softshell crabs, young butterfish, and multitudes of mussels and clams. I find great enjoyment in spending an early morning raking for clams or fishing for snappers, flounder, or "stripers." Along with farmstands popping up everywhere, there are the lesser-known but equally wonderful "backyard" providers of fresh eggs and fresh-killed poultry and game. And what to do with all of this bounty? The simpler the preparation techniques, the better—uncomplicated grilling, easy poaching, efficient steaming, light-handed flavoring, and, above all, masterfully simple presentation.

MENU · HEAD-ON SHRIMP IN TOMATO CHERVIL BROTH · ASPARAGUS SPEARS WITH DILL SHALLOT VINAIGRETTE · PINEAPPLE RASPBERRY NAPOLEON · SERVES 4

If you prefer to serve the entrée without the shrimp heads, save them to make a flavorful broth for soups and sauces. Wrapped tightly, they will keep in the freezer for up to one month. Serve the shrimp with a very fresh loaf of classic French bread—perfect for soaking up the broth. To create a healthful version of a Napoleon, I replace high-fat puff pastry with layers of thinly sliced pineapple. Use either Yogurt Cheese (page 15) or Enlightened Crème Fraîche (page 14), which should be prepared a day in advance.

Head-On Shrimp in Tomato Chervil Broth

1	28-ounce can whole tomatoes
¹/₂	cup dry white wine
14	sprigs of fresh chervil, 8 reserved for garnish
1	garlic clove, smashed
	Kosher salt and freshly ground black pepper
2	pounds head-on shrimp, submerged in cold water to clean (about 12)

SERVES 4

Place the tomatoes and their juice in a 3-quart pot and break them up with a fork. Add the wine, 6 sprigs of chervil, garlic, and 1 cup of water and bring to a boil. Reduce the heat and simmer 15 minutes. Pour the mixture into a fine-mesh strainer and let sit for 10 minutes. Discard the tomato pulp. Season with salt and pepper. Return the broth to the pot and bring to a boil. Add the shrimp, reduce the heat, and simmer for 2 to 3 minutes, or until the shrimp are pale pink and the tails curl.

Divide the shrimp among 4 shallow soup bowls. Ladle some of the broth into each bowl and garnish with the chervil.

ABOVE LEFT *To clean head-on shrimp, submerge them very briefly in water and remove with a slotted spoon.* **OPPOSITE** *Chervil infuses the broth with a hint of anise flavor. I like to soak up every bit of it with a piece of classic French bread.*

Asparagus Spears with Dill Shallot Vinaigrette

1¼ *pounds asparagus, trimmed and stems*
         peeled if thick (about 20 spears)
1   *large lemon, very thinly sliced*
         Kosher salt and freshly ground black
         pepper
¼   *cup Dill Shallot Vinaigrette (page 16)*
         Fresh dill, for garnish

SERVES 4

Place the asparagus spears in the top of a steamer over boiling water. Steam for 2 to 3 minutes for thin asparagus, 5 to 6 minutes for thick.

Meanwhile, arrange 4 lemon slices on each of 4 serving plates. Remove the asparagus from the steamer and season with salt and pepper. Divide the spears among the plates, drizzle the vinaigrette over the top, and garnish with the dill.

Pineapple Raspberry Napoleon

1   *small fresh pineapple*
½   *cup Enlightened Crème Fraîche (page 14)*
         or Yogurt Cheese (page 15)
1   *pint fresh raspberries*

SERVES 4

Using a large, very sharp knife, cut the top and bottom away from the pineapple and place it upright on a cutting board. Cut the rind away from top to bottom, rotating the pineapple 4 times to create a square. Slice the trimmed pineapple lengthwise into 6 even slices, cutting away the core as you slice. Stack the slices and cut them in half. Arrange a slice of pineapple on each of 4 dessert plates. Spread 2 teaspoons of Enlightened Crème Fraîche on each slice and top with raspberries to cover. Repeat twice to make 3 layers, ending with the raspberries.

ABOVE *Asparagus Spears with Dill Shallot Vinaigrette.* **RIGHT** *A unique Napoleon— layers of juicy pineapple sliced thin, dressed with creamy yogurt cheese, then dotted with red raspberries.*

MENU · COOL JICAMA SLAW · GOLDEN PAPAYA AND
CRAB SALAD · YOGURT CONES WITH KIWIS · SERVES 4

My idea of a spa menu—cool, clean, and refreshing. Jicama is a wonder vegetable. It is available year-round, delicious raw or cooked, low in calories, high in potassium, and keeps, uncut, in the refrigerator for up to three weeks. What's more, it's a great low-fat alternative to crackers—whether eaten with a splash of lime and a pinch of salt or spread with a favorite dip. Make the slaw first and let it sit at room temperature while you prepare the papaya dish. Scoop tangy nonfat yogurt into purchased waffle cones, garnish with kiwis, and eat while taking an after-dinner walk.

Cool Jicama Slaw

1   *jicama, peeled and julienned (about 4 cups)*

2   *teaspoons minced jalapeño pepper*

3   *tablespoons fresh orange juice*

1   *tablespoon fresh lime juice*

1   *teaspoon rice vinegar*

3   *tablespoons chopped fresh cilantro*
    Kosher salt and freshly ground black pepper

SERVES 4

Place the jicama in a mixing bowl. In a small bowl, whisk together 1 teaspoon of the jalapeño, the juices, vinegar, cilantro, and salt. Pour over the jicama, toss gently, and season with salt and pepper. Arrange the slaw on 4 salad plates, garnish with the remaining jalapeño, and serve.

Golden Papaya and Crab Salad

1   *pound lump crabmeat, picked over*

½ *pound sugar snap peas, strings removed (about 2 cups)*

½ *small red onion, chopped*

½ *cup Lime Caper Vinaigrette (page 17)*
    Kosher salt and freshly ground black pepper

2   *medium papayas, halved, seeds removed, and peeled*
    Lime wedges

SERVES 4

Place the crabmeat in a medium mixing bowl and, using a fork, break it into bite-size pieces. Add the peas and onion and combine well. Stir in the vinaigrette, salt and pepper, and toss to coat. Slice a small piece off of each papaya half along the rounded edge and place on a plate. Spoon one quarter of the crab mixture into each papaya half, garnish with lime wedges, and serve.

ABOVE *A culinary chameleon, jicama is cut into crisp, thin matchsticks, then shot through with minced jalapeño and tossed in a sweet-tart vinaigrette.* **OPPOSITE** *Golden Papaya and Crab Salad is a colorful main course.*

Yogurt Cones with Kiwis

2	kiwis, peeled, sliced crosswise, and quartered
1/4	cup fresh lime juice
2	cups vanilla nonfat yogurt
4	waffle cones

MAKES 4 CONES

In a small bowl, combine the kiwis and lime juice and toss to coat. Spoon ½ cup of yogurt into each cone and top each with the kiwis.

LEFT *The summer sunlight creates a pretty mosaic on my zinc-topped kitchen worktable and painted steel patio chairs. Jadeite salad plates, bakelite forks, celluloid knives, and playful antique linen napkins are perfect for a summer menu.* RIGHT *A green enameled steel egg carrier doubles as an ice cream cone service.*

MENU · COOL CUCUMBER AND DILL SOUP · QUICK PICKLED RADISHES AND PEPPERS · GRILLED BUTTERFISH · PINK MARGARITA SLUSHES · SERVES 4

This menu typifies the simplicity of summer eating. Butterfish used to be quite difficult to find—I had to make a special trip to the Chinese markets to buy them—but recently my fishmonger has been carrying them. They are aptly named—smooth and buttery with fine flaky white flesh—and very little fat. They're easy to eat whole, since they have relatively few bones. If you can't find butterfish, use pompano or mackerel. Quick pickling requires almost no effort and is such a simple way to enjoy the sour, briny flavor of the vegetables my mother used to spend hours pickling. They're especially delicious the day after they're made and will keep up to three days in the refrigerator.

Cool Cucumber and Dill Soup

3	cucumbers, 2 peeled, seeded, and chopped, and 1 coarsely chopped, for garnish
1$^{1}/_{3}$	cups low-fat yogurt
1$^{1}/_{3}$	cups low-fat milk
2	tablespoons roughly chopped fresh dill
$^{1}/_{2}$	teaspoon ground coriander
1	teaspoon fresh lemon juice
2	teaspoons chopped fresh flat-leaf parsley
1	tablespoon chopped fresh mint

SERVES 4

Process the cucumbers in a food processor until smooth. Add the remaining ingredients and pulse to combine. Chill the soup in the refrigerator until cold, about 1 hour.

Divide among 4 chilled soup bowls and garnish with the chopped cucumber.

Quick Pickled Radishes and Peppers

$^{1}/_{2}$	cup rice vinegar
2	tablespoons sugar
$^{1}/_{2}$	teaspoon kosher or pickling salt
10	whole black peppercorns, cracked
12	radishes, halved lengthwise
4	peperoncini or Tuscan pickled peppers

MAKES ABOUT 2$^{1}/_{2}$ CUPS

In a small nonreactive saucepan, combine the vinegar, sugar, salt, and peppercorns and simmer over medium-low heat, until dissolved, about 2 minutes.

Meanwhile, cook the radishes and peppers in boiling salted water for 2 minutes, until the radishes lose some of their color. Drain and place in a shallow dish. Pour the hot vinegar mixture over, let cool, and chill in the refrigerator for 15 minutes. These will keep, tightly covered in the refrigerator, for 3 days.

RIGHT *My opalescent blown-glass dessert bowls and saucers shimmer against the cool, quiet green of Cool Cucumber and Dill Soup.*

Grilled Butterfish

8   6- to 8-ounce whole butterfish, or
      pompano or mackerel
2   teaspoons extra-virgin olive oil
      Kosher salt and freshly ground black
      pepper
      Parsley sprigs, for garnish

SERVES 4

Prepare a stove-top griddle or outdoor grill with the rack set 1 inch above the coals. Allow the grill to get very hot.

Meanwhile, brush the butterfish with the olive oil and season with salt and pepper. Grill the butterfish about 3 minutes per side, until the fish just begins to flake. Arrange 2 butterfish on each of 4 dinner plates, garnish with the parsley, and serve.

Pink Margarita Slushes

4   cups cubed watermelon (about
      ¼ medium), seeds removed
3   tablespoons fresh lime juice
⅔   cup tequila, if desired, or orange juice
5   tablespoons sugar

MAKES 4 CUPS

In a blender, combine all the ingredients, fill with ice, and process until smooth. Pour into 4 tall clear glasses and serve.

OPPOSITE *The smooth and buttery texture, mild flavor, fine flaky flesh and low-fat content of butterfish make them an excellent choice for a healthy main course. Briny quick-pickled vegetables accompany the succulent char-grilled fish.* **BELOW** *Frothy margarita slushes get their pink tint from watermelon chunks.*

MENU · GRILLED PORTOBELLO PIZZAS · MIXED GREEN SALAD WITH YELLOW PEPPER VINAIGRETTE · POACHED NECTARINES IN CHAMOMILE GLACÉ · SERVES 4

Portobello mushrooms make the most delicious—and healthy—pizza "crust." Using the mushroom whole is very dramatic, and when topped with a very thin large square of the best-quality Parmigiano-Reggiano it is perfect. Use a vegetable peeler to shave the Parmigiano-Reggiano to make the thinnest slices possible. Save the stem ends of the portobellos to make flavorful soups and stocks. Find the very ripest nectarines for the gorgeous dessert.

Grilled Portobello Pizzas

12	cherry tomatoes, halved (about ½ pound)
4	teaspoons fresh thyme leaves
2	tablespoons extra-virgin olive oil
1	tablespoon Roasted Garlic (page 14) Kosher salt and freshly ground black pepper
8	portobello mushrooms, cleaned and stems trimmed (about 3 pounds)
4	1½ × 3-inch shavings Parmigiano-Reggiano cheese (about ½ ounce)
4	very thin slices prosciutto (about 1 ounce)
4	tablespoons Rough-Cut Basil Pesto (page 14)

SERVES 4

Prepare a stove-top griddle or outdoor grill.

Combine the tomatoes, thyme, 2 teaspoons of olive oil, the roasted garlic, and salt and pepper in a small bowl and toss. Set aside.

Brush the top and bottom of each mushroom with the remaining oil. Sprinkle with salt and pepper and grill until the mushrooms are tender, about 4 minutes per side. Place the mushrooms stem side up on a cutting board. Arrange an equal amount of the tomato mixture on 4 mushrooms. Top each with a shaving of Parmigiano-Reggiano. Arrange a slice of prosciutto on each of the remaining mushrooms and spread 1 tablespoon of the pesto on top of each prosciutto slice. Arrange 1 of each pizza on each of 4 dinner plates and serve.

RIGHT *An unusually long porcelain fish platter is the perfect serving tray for these mini pizzas. For casual main courses like this, I use ivory-handled celluloid forks and knives and blown ale glasses.*

Mixed Green Salad with Yellow Pepper Vinaigrette

4   *cups mixed greens (arugula, dandelion,*
        mustard, mizuna), washed and torn
        into bite-size pieces
4   *tablespoons Raw Yellow Pepper*
        Vinaigrette (page 16)

SERVES 4

Place the greens in a large bowl. Stir the dressing well, pour over the greens, and toss well to coat.

Poached Nectarines in Chamomile Glacé

3   *chamomile tea bags*
1/2 *cup sugar*
1   *whole vanilla bean, or 1/2 teaspoon*
        pure vanilla extract
4   *medium ripe nectarines*

SERVES 4

In a medium stockpot, combine the tea bags, sugar, and vanilla with 4 cups of water. Bring to a boil, reduce the heat to a simmer, and stir until the sugar is dissolved. Add the nectarines and cook for 2 minutes, or until the skins are slightly loosened. Using a slotted spoon, remove the nectarines to a bowl. Using a vegetable peeler or sharp paring knife, peel each nectarine, allowing the juices to collect in the bowl. Return the nectarines and collected juices to the poaching liquid and cook for 10 minutes more. Transfer the fruit to a plate. Using a slotted spoon, remove the tea bags and vanilla bean and discard. Raise the heat to high and cook the poaching liquid until it is reduced to a thick syrup, about 15 minutes. Place the nectarines in individual serving dishes and drizzle the glacé over each.

ABOVE *Simple greens are stunning piled in a generously proportioned wooden salad bowl and served with hand-turned sterling silver salad servers.* **OPPOSITE** *Juicy nectarines imbue the glacé with the most unbelievable color, which is even more dazzling served in a bright white enamel bowl. The red-rimmed teacup and saucer is part of my collection of diner china.*

MENU · CHILLED BUTTERMILK TOMATILLO SOUP ·
SUMMER BURRITO · SALSA CRUDA ·
ROASTED APRICOTS WITH DULCE DE LECHE · SERVES 4

Chilled Buttermilk Tomatillo Soup

2   teaspoons extra-virgin olive oil
1   medium-size onion, coarsely chopped
1   pound tomatillos, husked, rinsed, and
      quartered
2   garlic cloves, minced
1   jalapeño pepper, seeded and finely
      chopped
3   cups Chicken Stock (page 13) or
      low-sodium canned
1   teaspoon ground cumin, plus a pinch for
      garnish
2   tablespoons coarsely chopped cilantro,
      plus 4 sprigs for garnish
1   cup buttermilk
    Kosher salt and freshly ground black
      pepper

SERVES 4

Heat the olive oil in a medium saucepan over medium heat. Add the onion and cook until translucent, about 10 minutes. Reduce the heat if the onion begins to brown. Add the tomatillos, garlic, and jalapeño and cook for 5 minutes. Raise the heat to medium-high, add the chicken stock, cumin, and cilantro, and cook 10 minutes more. Remove from the heat and cool. Pour the mixture into the bowl of a food processor and purée until smooth. Add the buttermilk, salt, and pepper and pulse to combine. Transfer to a bowl and chill in the refrigerator. Ladle the soup among 4 bowls and garnish each with a cilantro sprig and the cumin.

LEFT *I like to float a few raw, rough-chopped tomatillos in bowls of Buttermilk Tomatillo Soup. When cooked, they lose their assertively astringent flavor and firm texture and become fruity and herbal. A sturdy, bright restaurantware bowl and French bistro spoon are understated enough to allow the alluring green soup to shine.*

The beauty of this menu is that all of the dishes can be easily packed and carried off to your favorite park bench or sand dune. Tomatillo Soup is the perfect antidote to prickly summer heat. Sharp and citrusy, yet smooth and refreshing, it seems especially good after a long day of work in the garden. Whenever the fruit in my fruit bowl is just past the point of ripeness, I roast it. I suggest apricots for dessert, but peaches, plums, and nectarines roast beautifully, too. The traditional version of *dulce de leche*, a Latin American sweet, is full of fat, but my slimmed-down version is almost custardlike and is a great low-fat alternative to heavy cream. It is delicious drizzled over just-picked strawberries, too.

Summer Burrito

2   8-ounce skinless, boneless chicken breasts
    Kosher salt and freshly ground pepper
3   limes, juiced
2   red bell peppers, halved and cored
2   green bell peppers, halved and cored
1   medium-size onion, peeled
4   large flour tortillas
1   Anaheim chili, seeded and minced
2   cups shredded romaine lettuce
2   ounces farmer or hoop cheese
1/4 cup loosely packed cilantro leaves
2   very ripe tomatoes, coarsely chopped

SERVES 4

Season the chicken with salt and pepper. Place in a shallow dish and spoon two-thirds of the lime juice over. Let sit for 15 minutes. Meanwhile, julienne the peppers and onion.

Prepare a stove-top griddle or an outdoor grill. Remove the chicken from the lime juice and discard the juice. Grill the chicken 5 minutes per side, or until the juices run clear when pricked at the thickest point. Remove to a cutting board to cool. Meanwhile, warm the tortillas on the grill, turning frequently until they begin to puff slightly, about 1 minute. Tear the chicken into thin strips.

Lay the tortillas on a clean surface. Beginning about a quarter of the way up the middle of the tortilla, layer equal amounts of each ingredient, ending with a drizzle of the remaining lime juice. Fold up the bottom quarter of each tortilla and roll away from you, tucking in the sides as you go. Serve seam side down.

Salsa Cruda

4   *large ripe tomatoes, finely chopped*
1   *large onion, finely chopped*
1   *small bunch of cilantro, minced*
    Juice of 2 to 3 limes
    Kosher salt and freshly ground black
      pepper

MAKES ABOUT 3 CUPS

Combine the tomatoes, onion, and cilantro in a bowl. Stir in the lime juice and season with salt and pepper. Serve with the burritos. This tastes best on the day it is made.

Roasted Apricots with Dulce de Leche

½   *cup sugar*
¼   *teaspoon cinnamon*
6   *fresh apricots, halved and pitted*
1   *teaspoon pure vanilla extract*
¼   *cup Dulce de Leche (page 15)*
¼   *cup Grand Marnier or fresh*
    orange juice

SERVES 4

Preheat the oven to 450°F. In a small bowl, whisk together the sugar and cinnamon. In another bowl, toss the apricots, vanilla, and Grand Marnier. Add the sugar mixture and toss. In a 9 × 11-inch roasting pan, place the apricots skin side down. Roast for 15 to 20 minutes, shaking the pan once or twice, until the apricots are fork-tender.

Meanwhile, make the Dulce de Leche. Arrange 3 apricot halves, along with the pan juices, on each of 4 dessert plates. Drizzle 1 tablespoon of Dulce de Leche over each. The apricots can be served warm or at room temperature.

OPPOSITE *Wrapped sandwiches are so popular in Manhattan right now that the craze has inspired dozens of tiny takeouts and casual lunch spots. They are no doubt inspired by the original—the flour tortilla—which I use to wrap around everything from Caesar salad to classic burrito combinations, as I do here.* **ABOVE** *Delicious warm or at room temperature, roasted apricots drizzled with my version of Dulce de Leche are exquisite on a Limoges honey dip plate. The napkins, finished in a tight whip stitch, are vintage linens from the 1950s.*

MENU · MY FAVORITE SUMMER SANDWICH · DOUBLE CABBAGE SLAW · WATERMELON SQUARES IN CAMPARI · SERVES 4

Tomato sandwiches of all kinds are a staple in my summer kitchen. My favorite version, packed with thickly sliced, juicy garden tomatoes, can be a bit messy to eat. If I am serving these sandwiches to friends, I cut each sandwich in half, without the top slice of bread, then cut the remaining bread slices in half and place them on top. It makes the sandwich easier to eat. Use thinly sliced bread and the higher-fat ingredients such as avocado sparingly. Make the slaw first and let it sit at room temperature since it tastes better the longer the flavors are allowed to develop. Of course, you can serve the watermelon the traditional way, rind on, in half circles and eaten out of hand—but when cut in squares, not only are the pieces the perfect size for dipping into Campari, but the presentation is dazzling.

My Favorite Summer Sandwich

8	slices of organic black bread or seven-grain bread
1/2	cup Red Pepper Coulis (page 15)
1	cup sprouts (sunflower, daikon, radish, clover, or alfalfa)
1	medium-size red onion, grilled or raw, thinly sliced
2	large tomatoes, each cut into 6 slices
1	medium-size ripe Hass avocado, peeled, halved, pit removed, and cut into 1/4-inch slices
	Kosher salt and freshly ground black pepper

MAKES 4 SANDWICHES

Spread each slice of bread with 1 tablespoon of the coulis. Divide the sprouts evenly among 4 of the slices. Arrange 2 onion slices and 3 tomato slices in an even layer over the sprouts. Arrange the avocado over the tomato and sprinkle with salt and pepper. Top with a slice of bread and serve.

RIGHT *I call this my cutting board menu because, along with a very sharp knife, it is the only kitchen tool I need to make this super summer dinner.*

Double Cabbage Slaw

½	*small purple cabbage, shredded*
½	*small green cabbage, shredded*
1	*teaspoon sugar*
½	*cup plain nonfat yogurt*
1	*tablespoon lemon juice*
¼	*cup poppy seeds*
	Kosher salt and freshly ground black pepper

MAKES 6 CUPS

Combine the cabbages in a large bowl. In a small bowl, whisk together the sugar, yogurt, and lemon juice. Spoon over the cabbage and toss to combine thoroughly. Sprinkle the poppy seeds into the bowl. Season with salt and pepper and serve. The slaw will keep, tightly covered, in the refrigerator for up to 2 days.

Watermelon Squares in Campari

1	*5- to 6-pound watermelon, halved lengthwise*
½	*cup Campari (optional)*

SERVES 4

Using a very sharp knife, slice the rind from the bottom of each watermelon half. The halves will now lay flat on a cutting board. Working from top to bottom, trim the rind from the watermelon flesh in 4 cuts, creating 2 large squares. Cut each square in half to make 4 smaller squares. Cut the squares vertically into thirds. Rotate counterclockwise and repeat the cut. Rotate once more counterclockwise and cut into thirds again. Place on dessert plates and serve each with 2 tablespoons of Campari, if desired.

ABOVE *When it is too hot to cook, I prepare this slaw of shredded purple and white cabbages tossed in sweetened yogurt and lemon juice and dotted with poppy seeds.* **OPPOSITE** *Simple watermelon becomes a dramatic dessert when cut into squares and set on a pink Depression glass dessert plate.*

95

MENU · SUGAR SNAP PEAS WITH MINT LEAVES · TOMATOES WITH ORRECHIETTE · ROUGH-CUT BREADSTICKS · BLUEBERRY SHORTCAKE · SERVES 4

My version of summer pasta. Don't bother making this unless you have the most delicious, perfectly ripe and juicy tomatoes, as the dish depends almost exclusively on this one ingredient. You must make this with pasta that will catch the delicious juices. I find that orrechiette does it the best, but farfalle, fusilli, and penne work well, too. Season the tomatoes with a pinch of salt as you chop to coax the juices from them.

Sugar Snap Peas with Mint Leaves

1	pound sugar snap peas, ends pinched off and strings removed (about 5 cups)
2	tablespoons Orange Vinaigrette (page 17)
1/2	cup tightly packed mint leaves
	Kosher salt and freshly ground black pepper

SERVES 4

Prepare a medium bowl of ice water. Blanch the peas in boiling salted water for about 20 to 30 seconds and refresh in the ice water to stop the cooking. Drain. Spoon the vinaigrette into a bowl, add the peas, mint, and salt and pepper and toss to coat. Divide among 4 salad plates and serve.

Tomatoes with Orrechiette

1	teaspoon extra-virgin olive oil
1	garlic clove, coarsely chopped
3	pounds tomatoes (combination of Roma and Holland, cut in wedges, and cherry and pear left whole)
1	sprig of fresh thyme
1/4	cup dry white wine
1/2	cup Chicken Stock (page 13) or low-sodium canned
	Kosher salt and freshly ground black pepper
12	basil leaves, stacked, rolled, and cut into fine strips
1	cup dried orecchiette, cooked al dente

SERVES 4

In a large skillet, heat the oil over medium heat. Add the garlic and fry until it begins to turn gold, about 1 minute. Increase the heat to medium-high and add the tomatoes and thyme. Cook, stirring gently, until the skin begins to loosen from the tomatoes, about 2 minutes. Add the wine and cook 1 minute more. Add the chicken stock and simmer about 2 minutes. Season with salt and pepper. Remove the thyme and ladle the tomatoes into serving bowls. Garnish with the basil leaves and pasta.

RIGHT *I often use herbs as one would salad greens—whole leaves tossed together with traditional salad ingredients. I've reinterpreted the classic pairing of peas and mint by leaving the mint leaves whole and using sugar snap peas.*

Rough-Cut Breadsticks

1   *12 × 2-inch loaf of bread*
1   *tablespoon extra-virgin olive oil*
     Kosher salt

MAKES 4 BREADSTICKS

Preheat the oven to 425°F. Slice the bread in quarters lengthwise. Place the 4 bread-sticks on a baking sheet and bake until golden brown, about 5 minutes. Drizzle oil over each breadstick and sprinkle with salt.

Blueberry Shortcake

1   *pint blueberries*
2   *tablespoons superfine sugar*
$^1/_3$ *cup plus 1 tablespoon all-purpose flour*
1   *teaspoon baking powder*
1   *tablespoon plus a pinch of granulated*
     sugar
     Kosher salt
2   *tablespoons cold butter, cut into small*
     pieces
2   *tablespoon low-fat buttermilk*
12   *almond slivers*
1   *cup vanilla nonfat yogurt*

SERVES 4

Preheat 375°F.

Combine the blueberries with the super-fine sugar and set aside.

In a mixing bowl, sift together the flour, baking powder, pinch of sugar, and pinch of salt. With a pastry blender or fork, fold in the butter, mixing until it resembles coarse meal. Add the buttermilk and blend with a fork just until combined. On a lightly floured surface, pat the dough into a 4-inch square. (It should be about ½ inch thick.) Cut 4 biscuits with a 2-inch cutter. Place on a parchment-lined baking sheet, sprinkle with sugar, and top each with 3 almond slivers. Bake for 15 minutes, until golden. Cut the biscuits in half. Add the yogurt to the blueberries and stir to com-bine. Place a quarter of the berries on top of one half of each biscuit, and top with the other biscuit halves.

OPPOSITE *When my garden is bursting with tomatoes, I switch their role in my pasta dishes. Quickly simmered to break down their skins and release every bit of juice, very ripe toma-toes are the canvas on which orrechiette and bright green summer basil are scattered. The long, whimsical breadsticks are made even more dramatic by serving them in a small glass like my Depression glass water tumbler.* **ABOVE** *I can't imagine a summer going by without making blueberry shortcake.*

MENU · LEAFY CHOPPED SALAD · GRILLED CHICKEN WITH RED PEPPER AND BASIL · CARAMELIZED CORN WITH SHALLOTS · GRILLED FRUIT PANINI WITH YOGURT CHEESE · SERVES 4

Perfect for feeding a houseful of hungry summer guests, this menu features ingredients that you are likely to have on hand. For the salad, choose whatever greens look freshest; the point is to combine greens with different textures and flavors. When preparing the marinade for the chicken, always reserve some before placing the chicken into it. Of course, I prefer using fresh corn kernels for the Caramelized Corn with Shallots, but frozen will do.

Leafy Chopped Salad

1   small head of Boston lettuce, coarsely
    chopped (about 4 cups)
2   celery stalks, coarsely chopped (about
    ½ cup)
1   medium cucumber, quartered
    lengthwise and chopped (about
    1 cup)
1   small bunch of chives, cut into 1½-inch
    pieces
2   tablespoons Chive Vinaigrette (page 17)
    Kosher salt and freshly ground black
    pepper

SERVES 4

In a medium bowl, combine all of the vegetables and drizzle with the Chive Vinaigrette. Toss to coat and season with salt and pepper.

LEFT *Chopped coarsely and dressed in a vinaigrette full of chives snipped from my herb garden, the most common vegetables—Boston lettuce, celery and cucumber—make a delicious starter.* **OPPOSITE** *Serving food family style doesn't have to lack style. Layering the dishes in this menu—the grilled chicken arranged on a bed of caramelized corn then draped with grilled red pepper and basil—is dramatic on a very large English ironstone serving tray.*

Grilled Chicken with Red Pepper and Basil

3   tablespoons fresh lemon juice
4   teaspoons balsamic vinegar
2   tablespoons extra-virgin olive oil
3   tablespoons Chicken Stock (page 13) or
      low-sodium canned
1   garlic clove, minced
1½   pounds skinless, boneless chicken
      breasts, trimmed of fat
2   red bell peppers
      Kosher salt and freshly ground black
      pepper
8   fresh basil leaves

SERVES 4

In a shallow dish, whisk together the lemon juice, vinegar, oil, stock, and garlic. Reserve 3 tablespoons. Add the chicken, turning to coat, and marinate for 20 minutes.

Meanwhile, prepare a stove-top griddle or outdoor grill. Grill the peppers, turning frequently, until charred and wrinkled, about 10 minutes. Remove to parchment paper to cool. Peel over the parchment paper, reserving the juices. Cut the peppers into ¼-inch strips and place in a bowl. Stir in the collected juices and the reserved marinade. Season with salt and pepper.

Grill the chicken until the juices run clear when pricked at the thickest point, about 4 minutes per side. Arrange the chicken over the Caramelized Corn with Shallots and spoon the pepper mixture on top. Garnish with the basil.

ABOVE *Shaved from the freshest ears of Silver-sweet corn, tossed with a little sugar, and cooked just long enough for its natural sugars to concentrate, caramelized summer corn-off-the-cob is one of my favorite ways to cook fresh kernels.* **OPPOSITE** *I have created dozens of versions of Italy's favorite snack food, panini, or little sandwiches, ever since I first tasted them there. Here, juicy slices of nectarines crowned with yogurt cheese, sandwiched between two tiny squares of bread and quickly grilled, make a gorgeous summer dessert.*

Caramelized Corn with Shallots

1	tablespoon unsalted butter
4	ears of fresh corn, kernels shaved from the cob (about 3 cups)
4	large shallots, cut into ¼-inch slices
	Pinch of sugar
	Kosher salt and freshly ground black pepper to taste
2	tablespoons fresh thyme leaves

SERVES 4

In a large skillet over medium heat, melt the butter. Add the corn, shallots, sugar, and salt and pepper. Cook, stirring occasionally to prevent burning, until the corn is caramelized, about 5 minutes. Stir in the thyme and cook 5 minutes more. Season with salt and pepper.

Grilled Fruit Panini with Yogurt Cheese

¼	cup Yogurt Cheese (page 15)
1½	teaspoons honey, plus more for drizzling
2	drops of pure vanilla extract
8	slices of very thinly sliced white bread, crusts removed
2	very ripe small nectarines, plums, or peaches, thinly sliced
	Butter-flavored cooking spray

SERVES 4

In a small bowl, stir together the Yogurt Cheese, honey, and vanilla until combined well. Spread about 1 tablespoon of the yogurt cheese mixture on 4 slices of bread. Arrange a layer of fruit over the cheese and top with the remaining slices of bread.

Heat a medium skillet over medium heat and spray with cooking spray. Cook the panini, 2 at a time, until golden, about 2 minutes per side. Transfer to a cutting board and repeat with the remaining panini. Halve each panini, divide among 4 dessert plates, and drizzle with additional honey.

102

MENU · COLD LENTIL SALAD · HOT SMOKED SALMON ·
SHAVED GOLDEN BEET SALAD ·
INDIVIDUAL PEACH PASTRIES · SERVES 4

Cold Lentil Salad

¹/₂ cup green lentils, rinsed and picked over

1 garlic clove, halved lengthwise

1 celery stalk, finely chopped (about ¹/₂ cup)

¹/₂ small red onion, finely chopped (¹/₄ cup)

¹/₂ cup flat-leaf parsley, finely chopped (about ¹/₂ cup)

3 tablespoons fresh lemon juice

1 tablespoon extra-virgin olive oil

1 teaspoon warm water

Kosher salt and freshly ground black pepper

MAKES 2 CUPS

Combine the lentils and garlic in simmering salted water for 10 minutes, or until the lentils are crisp-tender. Drain and run the lentils under cold water. Discard the garlic. In a bowl, toss together the lentils, celery, onion, and parsley. In a small bowl, whisk together the lemon juice, olive oil, and water. Drizzle over the lentils and stir gently to incorporate. Season with salt and pepper.

Hot Smoked Salmon

2¹/₄ cups white rice

3 tablespoons dried rosemary

3 tablespoons dried dill

1 pound salmon fillet, cut into 4-ounce pieces

Kosher salt and freshly ground black pepper

4 large radicchio leaves

¹/₄ cup Arugula Pesto (page 15)

SERVES 4

Fill a paella pan or flat-bottomed wok with enough rice to make a 1-inch layer. Mix the herbs into rice. Season the salmon with salt and pepper. On a grill rack or 8 skewers large enough to overhang the rim of the pan and sprayed with cooking spray, place the

fillets and cover with a dome-shaped lid. Cook the salmon over moderately low heat for about 15 minutes, or until firm to the touch. Place each fillet in a radicchio leaf and drizzle pesto over them.

Shaved Golden Beet Salad

4 golden beets, very thinly sliced

12 whole basil leaves

2 teaspoons extra-virgin olive oil

Kosher salt and freshly ground black pepper

SERVES 4

Combine all of the ingredients in a small bowl and toss to coat.

The smaller the golden beet, the more tender, which is best if eaten raw as in this salad. A mandoline or Japanese vegetable slicer is essential for slicing the beets as thin as possible. Of course, red, pink, white, and the two-toned chiogga are perfectly appropriate here. My no-nonsense smoking method—no wood chips or special equipment is needed—perfumes the salmon with just the right amount of smoky flavor. Keep the heat low to prevent the rice from charring and experiment with your favorite combination of herbs. Discard the rice mixture when you're finished.

OPPOSITE *I pulled out my summer whites for this menu—an ironstone tea bowl for the lentil salad, a French porcelain utility tray for the beet salad, and a deep English ironstone platter for the salmon.* **ABOVE** *I can create Cold Lentil Salad in no time from basic pantry ingredients.*

OPPOSITE *I created a smoker by filling a shallow pan with a mix of white rice and herbs and laying metal skewers across the diameter.* LEFT *Whisper-thin slices of golden beets are tossed with whole basil leaves.* BELOW *I always have phyllo dough in my freezer. It comes in handy when I must make dessert on a moment's notice, as I did this peach pastry. Any thinly sliced, very fresh fruit will do.*

Individual Peach Pastries

2 *phyllo sheets, covered with plastic wrap and a damp towel*
1 *tablespoon unsalted butter, melted*
2 *very ripe peaches, halved, pitted, quartered, and sliced ¼ thick*
8 *teaspoons light brown sugar*

MAKES 4 2 × 2-INCH PASTRIES

Preheat the oven to 400°F.

Remove one sheet of phyllo from under the wrap to a clean work surface. Brush it with half of the melted butter. Lay the second sheet of phyllo on top and brush with the remaining butter. Cut the phyllo in half lengthwise, then quarter lengthwise, to make 8 rectangles.

Place 4 of the rectangles on a baking sheet lined with parchment paper and sprayed lightly with nonstick cooking spray. Place the remaining rectangles on top of each, making four 4-layered pastries. Arrange about 10 to 12 peach slices on each pastry and sprinkle 1 teaspoon of brown sugar over each. Bake for 10 minutes. Remove from the oven and sprinkle each pastry with an additional teaspoon of brown sugar. Return to the oven and bake 5 to 7 minutes more, until the sugar has melted and is bubbly.

107

MENU · CORN CHOWDER · FARMSTAND SALAD WITH GRILLED TURKEY SAUSAGE · PEACH RASPBERRY SLUMP · SERVES 4

Fresh from the farmstand to the front porch, where eating supper in the waning summer sun is the rule. . . . These recipes were inspired by a hurried trip to my favorite farmstand and a house full of hungry summer guests. There are excellent low-fat sausages in the market now and I always have them on hand for occasions like this. Summer fruit desserts are quite simple to create—I combine peaches and raspberries and spoon biscuit dough on top.

Corn Chowder

3   slices ¼-inch-thick pancetta or slab bacon, cut into ½-inch pieces
1   medium-size onion, diced
2   medium-size russet potatoes, peeled and cut into 1-inch cubes
6   cups low-fat milk
4   ears of corn, kernels shaved from cob
1   tablespoon fresh thyme
     Kosher salt and freshly ground black pepper

SERVES 4

In a nonstick skillet over low heat, cook the pancetta until crisp and golden. Using a slotted spoon, transfer the pancetta to a paper towel and reserve. Remove all but 1 tablespoon fat from the skillet. Add the onion and sauté over medium-high heat until translucent, about 2 minutes. Add the potatoes and cook for 2 to 3 minutes. Do not brown. Add 1 cup of milk, reduce the heat to medium, and bring to boil, stirring often. Add the next 4 cups of milk 1 cup at a time, allowing it to come to a boil after each addition (about 30 minutes total). Add the corn with the final cup of milk and cook 15 minutes more. Stir in the thyme and season with salt and pepper. Garnish with the reserved pancetta, and serve.

Farmstand Salad with Grilled Turkey Sausage

6   cups mixed baby greens
6   radishes, thinly sliced
1   small zucchini, very thinly sliced
1   small summer squash, very thinly sliced
2   cups green beans, trimmed
2   carrots, thinly sliced
4   links of turkey or other low-fat sausage
4   ¾-inch-thick slices of country sourdough bread (optional)
4   tablespoons Buttermilk Dressing (page 15)

SERVES 4

Prepare a stove-top griddle or an outdoor grill.

In a large bowl, combine all of the vegetables and set aside. Grill the sausage until golden brown, about 5 to 7 minutes. Transfer to a cutting board and cut into ¼-inch pieces. Grill the bread until golden, about 2 minutes.

Toss the sausage into the salad bowl, drizzle the Buttermilk Dressing over, and toss to incorporate. Place a slice of grilled bread on each of 4 dinner plates and arrange the salad over each piece.

LEFT *Adding the milk in stages allows the base for Corn Chowder to become thick and creamy.* RIGHT *The Farmstand Salad can be tossed together before serving, but I love to spread the ingredients out on wooden cutting boards and let my guests compose their own salads right at the table.*

Peach Raspberry Slump

3	cups sliced peaches (about 5)
¾	cup raspberries
2	tablespoons light brown sugar
4½	tablespoons plus ½ teaspoon granulated sugar
2	teaspoons cornstarch
⅛	teaspoon cinnamon
¾	cup all-purpose flour
½	teaspoon baking powder
¼	teaspoon baking soda
	Pinch of kosher salt
2	tablespoons chilled unsalted butter, cut into pieces
2½	tablespoons plain nonfat yogurt
2	tablespoons skim milk
¼	teaspoon pure vanilla extract

SERVES 4

Preheat the oven to 400°F.

In a 9-inch pie pan, stir together the fruit, brown sugar, 2 tablespoons granulated sugar, the cornstarch, and cinnamon. In a bowl, stir together the flour, 2½ tablespoons granulated sugar, the baking powder, baking soda, and salt. With a fork, blend in the butter until the mixture resembles coarse crumbs. In a small bowl, whisk together the yogurt, milk, and vanilla and stir into the flour mixture until just combined.

Knead the dough lightly on a work surface and pat lightly until it is about ¾ inch thick. Drop the dough in 4 mounds over the fruit, sprinkle the remaining ½ teaspoon sugar over the dough, and bake in the middle of the oven until the biscuits are golden and cooked through, about 20 to 25 minutes.

ABOVE *Ordinary vegetables look extraordinary when sliced imaginatively, as the zucchini and summer squash are here.* **OPPOSITE** *Sometimes called a grunt, other times a slump, stewed summer fruit tucked beneath golden baked biscuits is a classic New England dessert.*

MENU · GRILLED SOFT-SHELL CRAB, CORN, AND ASPARAGUS WITH ARUGULA PESTO · GUAVA ON SHAVED ICE · SERVES 4

Silk and soak the corn, prepare the grill, and have dinner on the (picnic) table in under an hour. Guava is a funny-looking mottled fruit with a beautiful pink, sweet flesh. Serve it with small spoons so that you can scoop up every bit of it.

Grilled Soft-Shell Crab, Corn, and Asparagus with Arugula Pesto

4 *ears of fresh corn, husk attached, silks removed*
1 *bunch or 24 asparagus spears, ends trimmed*
³/₄ *cup Arugula Pesto (page 15)*
2 *tablespoons extra-virgin olive oil*
8 *soft-shell crabs*
   Kosher salt and freshly ground pepper
4 *cups mixed greens*

SERVES 4

In a large pot filled with cold water, soak the corn for 30 minutes. Blanch the asparagus in a large pot of boiling water and transfer to a bowl of ice water. Meanwhile, prepare the Arugula Pesto.

Prepare a stove-top griddle or outdoor grill. Grill the corn in the husk, turning occasionally, for 15 to 20 minutes. (If your grill has a cover, close it to allow the corn to steam.) Brush the asparagus with some of the olive oil and grill for 4 to 5 minutes, turning once or twice. Use a vegetable tray to prevent the asparagus from falling through the grill rack. Transfer the corn and asparagus to a large platter and serve with the Arugula Pesto. Grill the crabs until bright orange and slightly charred, about 2 to 3 minutes per side. Season with salt and pepper. Place the greens in a large salad bowl and set the crabs on top.

Guava on Shaved Ice

2 *cups shaved ice*
2 *ripe guavas, halved crosswise*

SERVES 4

Spoon ½ cup of shaved ice onto each of 4 rimmed dessert plates. Place a guava half in the center of each and serve.

LEFT *Casual food: plump asparagus spears and sweet yellow corn are meant for picking up with your fingers.* **ABOVE** *The best way to eat a guava is chilled, right out of the skin. For a dramatic presentation, I set it on a milk glass plate with shaved ice. The Victorian sterling silver spoons boast exquisite gold-washed bowls.* **RIGHT** *Soft-shell crabs plucked from the grill perfectly wilt tender mixed greens.*

MENU · FRESH BEAN SALAD · GRILLED STUFFED CALAMARI · GRILLED MANGOES WITH JALAPEÑO VINAIGRETTE · ROOT BEER FLOAT · SERVES 4

This menu boasts as many textures, flavors, and colors as a summer garden in full bloom. It is a very good example of how to effortlessly work plenty of fruits and vegetables into a daily diet. Toss fruit onto the grill and it becomes part of the entrée. If your experience with calamari is limited to the deep-fried or boiled preparations, my grilled version will be a revelation. Naturally tender, calamari has a reputation for being tough and chewy, which is really a result of overcooking. Calamari stuffed with tomatoes and cooked in a heavy sauce is popular all over the Mediterranean. When perfectly charred it needs little more than a generous squeeze of fresh lime. Summer without a root beer float? Never.

Fresh Bean Salad

1   pound mixed fresh beans (cranberry, wax, fava, lima, green), washed and picked over
2   tablespoons fresh lemon juice
1   teaspoon Dijon mustard
1   small shallot, thinly sliced
3   tablespoons extra-virgin olive oil
     Kosher salt and freshly ground black pepper

SERVES 4

Blanch the beans in boiling salted water. If using fava beans, slip off tough outer skins before blanching. Place the beans in a large bowl. In a small bowl, whisk together the lemon juice, mustard, shallot, olive oil, and salt and pepper. Drizzle over the beans and toss to coat.

Grilled Stuffed Calamari

2   large ripe tomatoes, seeded and diced
1½   heads frisée, coarsely chopped
2   teaspoons capers
2   tablespoons plus 1 teaspoon extra-virgin olive oil
1   lime, zested and juiced
     Kosher salt and freshly ground black pepper
½   pound squid, bodies only, rinsed and halved crosswise (about 8)

SERVES 4

Prepare a stove-top griddle or an outdoor grill. In a medium bowl, combine the tomatoes, frisée, and capers. In a small bowl, whisk together 2 tablespoons olive oil, lime juice and zest, and salt and pepper. Drizzle over the frisée mixture and toss to coat. Stuff 1 tablespoon of the frisée mixture into each squid. Brush the remaining teaspoon of olive oil on the squid. Grill for 5 to 7 minutes, turning frequently.

LEFT *Green, wax, and lima beans are lightly dressed in a mustard vinaigrette.* RIGHT *I first ate calamari prepared this way in Italy. I create different stuffings every time I make them, but among my favorites is summer tomatoes, feathery frisée, and briny capers. The squid look delectable in a featheredge creamware platter.*

Grilled Mangoes with Jalapeño Vinaigrette

2   mangoes, peeled, pitted, and sliced into
      ¹/₄-inch slices
2   tablespoons Jalapeño Vinaigrette
      (page 17)

SERVES 4

Prepare a stove-top griddle or outdoor
grill. Grill the mangoes until deep golden
and char marks are clear, about 2 minutes
per side. Transfer to a shallow dish. Drizzle the Jalapeño Vinaigrette over the mangoes and serve.

Root Beer Float

2   cups vanilla frozen yogurt
1   quart Barq's or Stewart's root beer

MAKES 1¹/₂ QUARTS

Scoop ¹/₂ cup frozen yogurt into each of 4
tall glasses. Add enough root beer to fill
each glass. Serve each with an iced tea
spoon and straw.

ABOVE *Mangoes are perfectly suited to grilling, their sweet flesh rich and sturdy enough to
stand up to a good charring.* **RIGHT** *Every time
I make this root beer float I think of the special
visits my father and I would make to an ice
cream stand when it was simply too hot to
work in the garden. I serve my version in old-
fashioned soda fountain glasses.*

MENU · SPARKLING FRUIT COOLERS · APRICOT-GLAZED CHICKEN · LAYERED SUMMER SALAD · CHERRY FRUIT SALAD · SERVES 4

This menu is perfect for an early-evening picnic on the porch. The Fruit Coolers are essentially a grown-up—and far healthier—version of the sticky, sweet fruit slushes I loved as a child. I keep a supply of fruit ice cubes in my refrigerator from Memorial Day to Labor Day. There are so many juices and nectars available—experiment with different combinations. The deliciously messy chicken is brushed with simple apricot glaze punctuated with hot pepper that produces a gorgeous amber lacquer when roasted. I highly recommend eating it with your hands.

Sparkling Fruit Coolers

1½ cups fresh lemonade, sweetened to taste
1½ cups fresh limeade, sweetened to taste
1½ cups fruit juice, such as cranberry,
        orange, apricot, or peach nectar
1   quart sparkling water
4   lime slices

MAKES 1 QUART

Freeze the lemonade, limeade, and juice in 3 or 4 ice cube trays. Fill each of 4 tall glasses to the top with an assortment of ice cubes and add sparkling water to fill. Garnish with limes and serve with iced tea spoons.

Apricot-Glazed Chicken

1   cup apricot jam
3   teaspoons dry mustard
1   tablespoon sherry vinegar
2   tablespoons extra-virgin olive oil
     Pinch of cayenne pepper
1   whole chicken, cut into parts (about
        6 pounds)
     Kosher salt and freshly ground black
        pepper

SERVES 4

Preheat the oven to 400°F.

In a small bowl, combine the jam, mustard, vinegar, olive oil, and cayenne. Season the chicken with salt and pepper, then brush with the glaze. Roast, basting with the glaze, for 10 minutes. Turn the chicken and roast for 10 minutes more. Baste the chicken with the glaze and roast 5 minutes more, or until the glaze is just crisp.

LEFT Hot or cold, Apricot-Glazed Chicken is ideal for packing into a picnic basket. Bring lots of napkins! **RIGHT** Fill a glass with cubes of frozen fruit juice and drench them in sparkling water for the ultimate cool, colorful summer drink.

Layered Summer Salad

1	large yellow bell pepper, julienned
2	tablespoons lemon juice
¼	cup extra-virgin olive oil
	Kosher salt and freshly ground black pepper
1	large red bell pepper, julienned
1	large orange bell pepper, julienned
20	radishes, very thinly sliced
6	medium carrots, finely shredded
2	tablespoons lime juice
2	tablespoons orange juice
2	tablespoons grapefruit juice
2	tablespoons raspberry wine vinegar

SERVES 4

In a medium bowl, combine the yellow pepper, lemon juice, and 1 tablespoon olive oil and toss to coat. Season with salt and pepper and transfer to a clear serving bowl. Repeat with remaining vegetables, tossing each in a different juice or vinegar and oil combination, spreading each in a thin layer in the bowl.

Cherry Fruit Salad

1	pint raspberries
1	pint blueberries
½	pound Bing cherries
2	medium oranges, peeled, pith removed
2	tablespoons eau de vie

In a large bowl, combine the blueberries and raspberries. Working over parchment paper, pit the cherries, discard the pits, and add the fruit to the berry mixture. Section the oranges and add them to the bowl. Pour the juices that have collected on the paper into the bowl, add the eau de vie, and gently toss. Divide among four bowls and serve.

ABOVE *For dessert, I like to serve bowls of summer fruits splashed with eau de vie.* **LEFT** *A great dish to bring to a party, Layered Summer Salad is simple to make and stunning to look at.*

FALL

This is the season of intense flavors, assertive spices, and frost-sweetened produce. The mature home garden and the overflowing farmers' markets are full of some of the most healthful foods of the year: brassica, squashes, and root vegetables that are sweeter, crisper, and more colorful than ever before. The cool weather encourages us to spend more time in the kitchen experimenting with techniques and ingredients. Wilting, roasting, mashing, pureeing, caramelizing—these are the healthful cooking techniques I use to create simple, mouthwatering dishes from the season's freshest ingredients. Roasting an eggplant or a squash intensifies its best qualities so it easily can be transformed into a delicious first course, a soup, or a main course vegetable, a puree. In autumn, our palates crave sturdier textures and more dramatic flavors. A dry, spicy marinade, or rub, changes the character of a boneless pork loin, and a lacquered pomegranate sauce for rack of venison makes use of an esoteric but highly interesting and nutrient-rich fruit. Elusive Indian spices, Spanish saffron, Israeli couscous, and Japanese miso are just a few of the surprising yet widely available ingredients you will find in the following menus. Autumn desserts, although incredibly easy to make, fulfill an important place in each of the menus; some are tart, some are savory, some are cooked, some are simply fresh fruit—but all are sweet and delectable.

MENU · **GIANT ROASTED CARROTS** · TANDOORI-SPICED FLANK STEAK · **SPICED OKRA** · FROZEN CHAI · SERVES 4

Flank steak is one of the least fatty, therefore less tender, cuts of meat, but a quick soak in a strong, spicy marinade flavors and tenderizes the meat without any added fat. Curry paste, which is available in a range of heat intensities, should be used to taste. Large carrots take center stage in this menu, their size perfect for sustaining the high heat of roasting—they won't shrivel—and their nutrition profile top-notch. Chai is an invigorating spiced tea drunk by porters on rigorous treks in the mountains of Nepal. My frozen version never fails to take me back to the mountains where I first tasted it.

Giant Roasted Carrots

8	large carrots, peeled
1/4	cup tamarind chutney
1/2	teaspoon curry powder
1/2	teaspoon ground coriander
	Kosher salt

SERVES 4

Preheat the oven to 400°F.

Place the carrots in a 9 × 13-inch roasting pan. In a small bowl, whisk together the chutney, curry powder, coriander, and 1 cup of water. Add salt to taste. Pour the mixture over the carrots and cover the pan tightly with aluminum foil. Roast for 30 minutes, shaking the pan occasionally, until the carrots are fork-tender. Raise the heat to 475°F., remove the foil, and roast 7 to 10 minutes more.

Tandoori-Spiced Flank Steak

1	pound flank steak, trimmed of fat
2	tablespooons tamari
1/4	cup honey
1	tablespoon tandoori spice
1	tablespoon red curry paste

SERVES 4

Place the steak in a shallow baking dish. In a small bowl, mix the tamari, honey, tandoori spice, and curry paste. Brush the mixture on the steak and let sit at room temperature for 45 minutes or overnight in the refrigerator. Turn once or twice.

Prepare a stove-top griddle or outdoor grill. Grill the steak 5 to 7 minutes per side. Transfer to a cutting board to rest for 5 minutes. Cut the steak into 1/4-inch slices and divide among 4 dinner plates.

ABOVE *Indian spices lend this menu their generous warmth and autumnal color. Fiery orange curry paste and tandoori spice enliven the flank steak, blazing yellow turmeric coats the okra, and soft golden curry powder brightens the carrots.* **RIGHT** *My brown transferware undertray seems to be custom made for these long golden roasted carrots.*

Spiced Okra

$1/2$	teaspoon ground cumin
$1/2$	teaspoon ground coriander
1	teaspoon turmeric
1	teaspoon mustard seeds
4	dried red pepper flakes
1	medium-size onion, diced
$1^3/4$	cups fresh okra, cut into thirds on a bias
$1/2$	cup plain nonfat yogurt

SERVES 4

In a heated wok, combine the cumin, coriander, turmeric, mustard seeds, and pepper flakes and cook, stirring with a wooden spoon, until the mustard seeds pop, about 2 minutes. Add the onion and cook for 2 minutes more, until the onion is soft and translucent. Turn the heat to high and add the okra. Cook, stirring occasionally, until it is bright and gives slightly when pressed with the spoon, about 2 minutes. Serve with yogurt for dipping.

Frozen Chai

1	4-inch piece of fresh ginger, peeled and coarsely chopped
$1/2$	cup honey
2	tablespoons loose jasmine tea or 6 tea bags
1	cup skim milk

MAKES 1 QUART

In a 2-quart saucepan, combine the ginger with 4 cups of water. Bring to a boil, reduce the heat, and simmer 20 minutes. Stir in the honey. Place the tea or tea bags in the liquid and steep for 3 minutes. Add the skim milk and bring to a boil. Remove from the heat, strain, and chill in an ice bath. Pour into an ice cream maker and follow the manufacturer's instructions. Alternatively, pour into a shallow freezerproof pan and freeze for 2 hours. Break up the chai with a fork and refreeze for 2 hours. Spoon into the bowl of a food processor and process until smooth. Refreeze for 1 hour more. The chai will have the consistency of shaved ice.

RIGHT *The warmest frozen dessert: honey, ginger, jasmine tea, and milk.*

MENU · ENDIVE AND WATERCRESS SALAD WITH
QUICK PICKLED RED ONIONS · WILD RICE WITH DRIED FRUIT ·
THYME-ROASTED POUSSIN · CARAMELIZED APPLES IN
PHYLLO TARTS · SERVES 4

A very long time ago, I asked one of the butchers at Mercurios Butchers in Fairfield, Connecticut, how he trussed the beautiful poussins that line his meat case. I've been using his method ever since. The rice dish is really my version of pilaf. Rather than browning the rice in butter, I cook it like pasta, in plenty of water, then drain it. I sweat the leeks in a tiny amount of butter, then toss everything together. Studded with dried fruits and leeks, it boasts the mosaic look and texture of a classic pilaf. Phyllo is neither the culinary bully nor nutrition nightmare that it is commonly thought to be. Quick hands and a good pastry brush or nonstick cooking spray are all you need to make delicous pastries. You can use muffin tins for the tart shells or make a single tart in a 6-inch cake pan.

Endive and Watercress Salad with Quick Pickled Red Onions

1	medium-size red onion, very thinly sliced (about 1 cup)
2	tablespoons fresh lemon juice
	Kosher salt and freshly ground black pepper
2	large endives (about 2 cups)
2	small bunches of baby watercress, tough stems removed (about 4 cups)
1	tablespoon extra-virgin olive oil
2	ounces fresh goat cheese, crumbled

SERVES 4

In a small bowl, combine the onion, lemon juice, and a pinch of salt and pepper and set aside.

Meanwhile, chop the endives in a cross-hatched fashion, beginning at the base and working to the point. Place the endive and watercress in a large bowl. With a slotted spoon, transfer the onion to the bowl of greens. Whisk the oil in a steady stream into the lemon juice, pour over the greens, and toss, until coated well. Divide the salad among 4 plates and crumble the goat cheese on top.

Wild Rice with Dried Fruit

4	ounces wild rice (1/2 cup plus 2 tablespoons)
	Kosher salt and freshly ground black pepper
1	teaspoon extra-virgin olive oil
1	small leek, trimmed, well washed, and cut into 1/4-inch rounds (about 2/3 cup)
6	tablespoons Chicken Stock (page 13) or low-sodium canned
1/3	cup dried cranberries
1/4	cup chopped dried pears

SERVES 4

In a 2-quart pot of boiling salted water, add the rice and cook until the grains begin to puff and break open, about 40 minutes to 1 hour. Drain and refresh in cold water. Season with salt and pepper.

Heat the oil in a 2-quart saucepan. Add the leek and cook for 1 minute. Add 3 tablespoons of the stock, the cranberries, and pears and cook, covered, stirring occasionally, until soft, about 8 minutes. Add the rice and remaining stock, raise the heat to high, and cook, stirring, 1 to 2 minutes. Season with salt and pepper and serve.

Thyme-Roasted Poussin

4	12- to 14-ounce poussins
	Kosher salt and freshly ground pepper
1	teaspoon extra-virgin olive oil
1	lemon, quartered
12	large sprigs of thyme
12	sprigs of marjoram
4	garlic cloves, crushed
2	tablespoons Cognac

SERVES 4

Preheat the oven to 500°F.

Rinse the poussins and season the cavities with salt and pepper. Rub each with 1/4 teaspoon olive oil. Fill each cavity with a lemon wedge, 2 sprigs each of thyme and marjoram, and 1 crushed garlic clove. Loosen the skin from the breast of each poussin. Slide a sprig each of thyme and marjoram between the skin and the breast. Spoon the Cognac (1/2 tablespoon per bird) into the breast pockets of each poussin. Truss with kitchen string. On a roasting rack set in a roasting pan, roast for 30 minutes, or until the juices run clear when the thigh is pierced with a fork.

OPPOSITE *Four poussins fit perfectly in my handsome French copper skillet.* **ABOVE** *I have two requirements for my salads: ingredients well chosen and greens well dressed. The combination of creamy goat cheese, crisp endive, peppery watercress, and tart pickled onions is one of the very best.*

129

ABOVE *1. Thyme-Roasted Poussin mis en place. 2. Season a poussin, then stuff with garlic, thyme, marjoram, and lemon. 3. Create a pocket between the skin and breast meat; spoon in the cognac. 4. Hold the ends of a 12-inch piece of string between your thumbs and forefingers, creating a U shape. Run the string underneath the shoulders of the poussin, up over the breasts, and along the inside of the thighs. Draw the string underneath and around the feet. 5. Join the string ends and tie a knot, drawing the feet together. 6. Lay the poussin breast-side-down. Draw the string ends around the feet again and tie them together in a knot. 7. Repeat with remaining poussins. 8. Place the poussins breast-side-up in a roasting pan large enough to allow space between each. 9. Set the roasted poussin over the wild rice and serve.* **OPPOSITE** *My vintage pressed glass cakestand makes an ideal serving platter for Caramelized Apples in Phyllo Tarts.*

Caramelized Apples in Phyllo Tarts

3	sheets of phyllo, thawed if frozen
2	teaspoons plus 1 tablespoon sugar
2	McIntosh or other firm apples, peeled and cut into ½-inch wedges
1	tablespoon fresh lemon juice
¼	cup apple juice
1	tablespoon butter, plus 2 teaspoons melted butter, for brushing phyllo
1	tablespoon Cognac or apple juice
	Pinch of ground ginger
	Pinch of cinnamon
	Finely chopped crystallized ginger

SERVES 4

Preheat the oven to 350°F. On a work surface, stack the phyllo sheets and cut out four 7-inch squares (12 total), discarding the scraps. Stack the squares between 2 sheets of wax paper and cover with a kitchen towel.

Spray the countertop and 4 individual ring molds with nonstick cooking spray. Lay a square of phyllo on the counter and sprinkle with some of the 2 teaspoons of sugar; lay a second square on top, brush with the melted butter, and sprinkle with sugar. Cover with a third layer and sprinkle with sugar. Work the phyllo into the ring mold as you would a handkerchief into a pocket, letting the edges overhang. Repeat with the remaining phyllo. Place the molds on a parchment-lined baking sheet and bake for 10 to 12 minutes, or until golden brown. Carefully transfer the phyllo shells to a rack.

Combine the apples, lemon juice, and apple juice and set aside. In a nonstick skillet, melt the butter over medium heat. Add 1 tablespoon sugar and caramelize for 3 minutes, or until golden brown. Remove from the heat, add the Cognac, and stir with a wooden spoon. Return the pan to the heat, add the spices and apple mixture, and cook, stirring occasionally, until the apples are tender, about 5 minutes. Divide the apples among the shells and sprinkle with crystallized ginger.

MENU · HERBED STRIPED BASS · STEAMED BABY SPINACH · CELERY ROOT AND APPLE PURÉE · LEMON PUDDING CAKE · SERVES 4

Egg whites are excellent, no-fat dredging mediums. Use soft, leafy herbs on the bass; they form a pleasantly crisp coat when seared. Celery root or celeriac has a much milder flavor than its more common varietal cousin, bunch celery. Like jicama, it is very versatile and can be served raw cut into matchsticks for dipping or tossed in a light dressing or cooked into all manner of dishes. My favorite preparation, however, is celery root puréed with crisp, sweet Fuji apples.

Herbed Striped Bass

1	cup mixed fresh soft herbs (sage, parsley, basil, chives), coarsely chopped
	Kosher salt and freshly ground black pepper
4	4-ounce striped bass or rockfish fillets, skin off
1	egg white, lightly whisked

SERVES 4

Spread the herbs and salt and pepper on a large platter. Brush each fillet with the egg white, then dredge in the herbs. In a large nonstick skillet over medium-high heat, sear the fillets 3 to 4 minutes per side, or until cooked through and the flesh just begins to flake.

Steamed Baby Spinach

2	pounds baby spinach, stems trimmed
¼	cup fresh lemon juice
	Kosher salt and fresh ground black pepper
	Lemon wedges, for garnish

SERVES 4

Bring a large pot of salted water to a boil. Meanwhile, wash the spinach in cold running water. Place the spinach in a steamer and plunge into the boiling water for 1 minute, or until the spinach wilts. Transfer to a colander to drain. Arrange the spinach on a serving platter and season with the lemon juice and salt and pepper. Garnish with lemon wedges and serve.

Celery Root and Apple Purée

4³⁄₄	cups apple juice
1	cinnamon stick
1	bay leaf
2	medium celery roots (1 pound total), trimmed and coarsely chopped
8	firm, crisp apples such as Granny Smith or Fuji, peeled, cored, and chopped
1	tablespoon cider vinegar
	Kosher salt and fresh ground black pepper

SERVES 4

In a 2-quart saucepan, combine 3 cups of the apple juice, the cinnamon stick, and the bay leaf and bring to a boil. Add the celery root and cook for 15 minutes, until the liquid is reduced to a slightly thick syrup. Using a slotted spoon, remove the bay leaf and cinnamon stick. Add the apples, the remaining apple juice, and the vinegar and cook 5 to 7 minutes more, or until the liquid is completely reduced. Spoon the mixture into the bowl of a food processor and process until smooth. Season with salt and pepper and serve.

RIGHT *The subtle shimmer of antique silver lustreware dinner plates reflects beautifully on the soft whites, deep greens, and warm golds of Herbed Striped Bass, Steamed Baby Spinach, and Celery Root and Apple Purée.*

Lemon Pudding Cake

¹/₃ *cup sugar, plus additional for molds*

2 *tablespoons honey*

1 *large egg*

1¹/₂ *tablespoons butter, softened*

2 *teaspoons grated lemon zest*

2 *tablespoons all-purpose flour*

³/₄ *cup skim milk*

¹/₄ *cup well-shaken buttermilk*

¹/₄ *cup fresh lemon juice*

3 *large egg whites*

 Pinch of kosher salt

RASPBERRY SAUCE

1 *pint raspberries*

3 *teaspoons superfine sugar*

SERVES 4

Preheat the oven to 350°F. Spray an 8-inch glass pie dish with cooking spray and sprinkle with some sugar. In a bowl, beat the ¹/₃ cup sugar, honey, egg, butter, and lemon zest on medium speed about 2 minutes. Add the flour and beat until smooth. Add the milk, buttermilk, and lemon juice and beat until combined. In another bowl, using clean, dry beaters, beat the egg whites with the salt until soft peaks form, about 2 minutes. Stir about one third of the egg whites into the batter and gently fold in the rest. Spoon the batter into the prepared pie dish and place in a 9 × 11-inch baking pan. Add enough warm water to the pan to come halfway up the sides of the pie dish. Bake for 30 minutes, or until the pudding is browned lightly. Transfer the pudding to a wire rack to cool slightly.

Meanwhile, make the raspberry sauce. Combine one quarter of the berries with 1 tablespoon of water and 2 teaspoons of the superfine sugar and mash with the back of a spoon. Sprinkle the remaining sugar over the rest of the berries, then stir in the mashed berries and set aside for 30 minutes. Spoon the mixutre over each serving of pudding cake and serve.

ABOVE *Lemon Pudding Cake is exquisite on a Depression glass plate.* **LEFT** *Herbed Striped Bass, Steamed Baby Spinach, and Celery Root and Apple Purée.* **OPPOSITE** *A successful— and healthful—way to prepare spinach is to steam it, then shower it with fresh lemon juice.*

MENU · ROASTED SWEET POTATOES WITH PINEAPPLE
CRANBERRY CHUTNEY · ESCAROLE HEARTS WITH LEMON
PUMPKIN SEED VINAIGRETTE · FROZEN YOGURT WITH PINK
PEPPERCORNS · SERVES 4

Roasted Sweet Potatoes with Pineapple Cranberry Chutney

| 4 | *medium-size sweet potatoes, scrubbed* |
| 1 | *cup Pineapple Cranberry Chutney (page 15)* |

SERVES 4

Preheat the oven to 425°F. Place the potatoes in a roasting pan and roast 45 minutes, until they yield easily to a knife. Halve each potato, place 2 halves on a dinner plate, and spoon ¼ cup of the chutney on top.

Escarole Hearts with Lemon Pumpkin Seed Vinaigrette

¼	*cup pumpkin seeds*
¼	*cup extra-virgin olive oil*
3	*tablespoons lemon juice*
	Kosher salt and freshly ground black pepper
2	*heads of escarole, tough outer leaves trimmed*
1	*cup loosely packed whole leaf cilantro*

Loaded with vitamins A and C, sweet potatoes are a nutritionist's dream. Roasted and served with a healthy, low-fat topping, they become a very satisfying meal. The sweet chutney is also a delicious accompaniment to roasted meats. The texture and flavor of the escarole hearts complement the pumpkin-seed-studded vinaigrette. Wrap the escarole leaves in damp paper towels and reserve for another use. For dessert, serve small cups of frozen yogurt dotted with pink peppercorns—which are not peppercorns at all but dried berries from a rose plant cultivated in Madagascar.

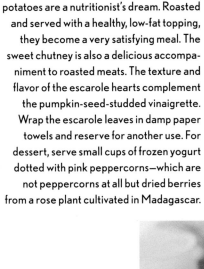

In a large skillet over high heat, toast the pumpkin seeds until they pop. Remove the skillet from the heat and add the olive oil. Whisk in the lemon juice. Season to taste with salt and pepper.

Cut the escarole on the bias, dividing each heart into 2 servings. Place a half on each of 4 salad plates and top with ¼ cup cilantro. Drizzle with the salad dressing and serve.

Frozen Yogurt with Pink Peppercorns

| 1 | *pint vanilla frozen yogurt* |
| 1 | *tablespoon pink peppercorns* |

SERVES 4

Divide the frozen yogurt among 4 dessert bowls. Garnish with the pink peppercorns and serve.

LEFT *Roasted to perfection, soothing sweet potatoes are filled with a sweet, spicy chutney.* **ABOVE** *Pungent and floral, pink peppercorns are pretty sprinkled on top of frozen yogurt.* **OPPOSITE** *Crunchy escarole hearts and an extra-tart vinaigrette with golden toasted pumpkin seeds balance beautifully with the creamy-textured sweet potatoes.*

137

MENU · CURRIED TOMATO SEAFOOD BOUILLABAISSE · SAFFRON RICE · PINK AND ORANGE PAPAYA WEDGES · SERVES 4

This version of bouillabaisse features white fish only. If you like, use a combination of fish and shellfish. When I use shrimp, I make a superb stock with the shrimp shells by roasting them in the oven, then deglazing the pan with a little white wine. I combine this with water, carrots, celery, and herbs and simmer for up to 1 hour, strain, cool, and freeze the stock. Saffron is traditionally used to perfume bouillabaisse, but I like to add a layer of fragrance and color to aromatic basmati. If you don't have saffron, use turmeric (Indian saffron) instead. Low in calories and a rich source of vitamin C, potassium, and fiber, papaya is a nutrition bargain. The yellow-orange-fleshed Solo is available nationwide, while the pink-fleshed Sunrise may be a bit trickier to find. They both boast the same nutritional profile and are equally delicious.

Curried Tomato Seafood Bouillabaisse

1	28-ounce can whole tomatoes
1/2	teaspoon cardamom seeds
2	whole cloves
1	1-inch stick cinnamon
1	whole dried red pepper or 1 1/2 teaspoons crushed red pepper
2	tablespoons curry powder
1	lemongrass stalk, cut into 1-inch pieces
1	pound assorted firm white fish (monk, halibut, black, tile), cut into 2-inch chunks
	Kosher salt
1/4	cup coarsely chopped parsley leaves

SERVES 4

In a large stockpot, combine the tomatoes, cardamom, cloves, cinnamon, red pepper, curry powder, and lemongrass with 6 cups of water and bring to a boil. Reduce the heat and simmer 20 minutes. Strain the broth. Add the fish to the broth and poach until opaque, about 10 minutes. Season with salt. Ladle into shallow soup bowls and garnish with the parsley.

Saffron Rice

2	pinches of saffron, crumbled
1/4	cup boiling water
1	cup basmati rice
	Kosher salt and freshly ground black pepper

SERVES 4

In a small bowl, combine the saffron and boiling water and steep for 5 minutes. Meanwhile, rinse the rice under cold water. Place the rice, 1 3/4 cups water, and saffron in a pot and bring to a boil. Reduce the heat to low and simmer, covered, for 20 minutes, until all the liquid is absorbed. Remove from the heat and let sit, covered, for 10 minutes. Fluff with a fork, season with salt and pepper, and either spoon into the bouillabaisse or serve on the side.

OPPOSITE *Saffron rice glows in one of my favorite pieces, a hammered copper rice pot. A beautifully shaped, shallow burnished bowl complements the fiery red Curried Tomato Seafood Bouillabaisse.*

Pink and Orange Papaya Wedges

1	Sunrise papaya
1	Solo papaya
	Fresh lime juice

Peel the papayas with a vegetable peeler. Halve, scoop out the seeds, and cut into 6 wedges. Place a wedge of each papaya on each of 4 dessert plates. Coursely chop the remaining papaya for garnish. Drizzle the lime juice over the wedges and serve.

TOP LEFT *A pinch of brilliant burnt-orange saffron, the stigmas of small purple crocuses, gives a dish a slightly bitter and floral flavor.* LEFT *Surprisingly simple to prepare, Curried Seafood Bouillabaisse is spooned over Saffron Rice and served in a stoneware bowl.* RIGHT *The colors of autumn are woven throughout this menu, and dessert is no exception. Pink and Orange Papaya Wedges reflect the colors of fall leaves at their peak.*

MENU · STEAMED BRUSSELS SPROUTS · MASHED RUTABAGAS · ROASTED RACK OF VENISON WITH POMEGRANATE SAUCE · SEARED APPLES · SERVES 4

I created this menu to satisfy my occasional craving for meat and potatoes. Venison is naturally lean—it has no internal fat—and is especially suited to a quick high-heat roast. The coating's assertive mix of juniper berries and Szechwan and black peppercorns locks in the meat's juices. Each chop is drizzled with a ruby-red sauce made from the pan juices and sweet-tart pomegranate juice, available in specialty and gourmet stores. Rather than serving expected mashed potatoes, I use nutritious rutabagas, mashing them with buttermilk and seasoning them with a dash of nutmeg. Steam the vitamin-rich Brussels sprouts until they are fork tender, and use the best balsamic vinegar you have for tossing. Don't be put off by the cooking time for the dessert; simply allow the seared apples to simmer while you eat the main course.

Steamed Brussels Sprouts

1	pound Brussels sprouts, trimmed and washed
2	teaspoons chopped fresh thyme
1	tablespoon balsamic vinegar
	Freshly cracked black peppercorns

SERVES 4

Blanch the Brussels sprouts in a large pot of lightly salted boiling water until tender, about 10 to 12 minutes, and refresh in cold water. Cut in half and transfer to a bowl. Add the thyme, vinegar, and pepper, toss to coat, and serve.

Mashed Rutabagas

2	small rutabagas, trimmed and cut into chunks
1/2	cup milk
1/4	cup buttermlk
1/4	teaspoon balsamic vinegar
	Dash of freshly grated nutmeg
	Kosher salt and freshly ground black pepper

SERVES 4

In a pot of boiling salted water, cook the rutabagas until fork-tender, about 15 minutes. Drain and mash using a large fork. Add the milk, buttermilk, vinegar, and nutmeg and mash until smooth. Season with salt and pepper and serve.

Roasted Rack of Venison with Pomegranate Sauce

1	tablespoon juniper berries
1	tablespoon Szechwan peppercorns
1	tablespoon black peppercorns
1	tablespoon dried thyme
1/4	rack of venison, 4 chops (about 2 pounds)
1/2	cup pomegranate juice
	Kosher salt
	Parsley, for garnish

SERVES 4

Preheat the oven to 425°F.

Combine the juniper berries, Szechwan and black peppercorns, and thyme in a resealable plastic bag and crush underneath a heavy cast-iron skillet. Rub all over the rack of venison. Place in a roasting pan and roast for 25 minutes. Remove to a cutting board to rest.

Meanwhile, skim the fat from the pan, place the pan on the stovetop, and turn the heat to high. Add the pomegranate juice and bring to a boil, scraping the bits from the sides of the pan until the liquid is reduced to a thick syrup. Add salt to taste. Carve the rack into 4 chops and arrange among 4 dinner plates. Drizzle the pomegranate sauce over each chop and garnish with the parsley.

RIGHT *Encrusted in a personality-packed rub, Roasted Rack of Venison glistens on a simple ironstone serving platter.*

Seared Apples

¹⁄₄   cup almonds

³⁄₄   teaspoon chopped candied ginger

¹⁄₂   teaspoon cinnamon

¹⁄₄   teaspoon nutmeg

¹⁄₄   cup (packed) light brown sugar

2   Gala or McIntosh apples, halved and
    cored

1   egg white

1   tablespoon butter

1³⁄₄   cups prune juice

SERVES 4

Preheat the oven to 350°F.

In a dry skillet over medium-high heat, toast the almonds until light golden brown and fragrant, stirring frequently. Let cool and grind into a fine powder.

Combine the almonds, ginger, cinnamon, nutmeg, and brown sugar in a shallow dish. Brush the apples with the egg white and press into the spice mixture.

Heat the butter in a saucepan over medium heat. Brown the cut side of the apples in the pan for 1 to 2 minutes. Turn the apples over and add ½ cup of water and the prune juice. Bring to a boil, then simmer for 1 hour, or until the apples are tender and the sauce is reduced to a thick syrup. Place an apple half on each of 4 dessert plates and spoon the sauce over each.

ABOVE *Halved and pressed into a fragrant mix of candied ginger and toasted nuts, Seared Apples are a sophisticated—and far healthier— version of those sticky sweet candied apples from childhood.* **LEFT** *The flavors of fall: roasted venison, Brussels sprouts, and mashed rutabagas.* **OPPOSITE** *Brussels sprouts are quickly sautéed in a bit of olive oil, finished with a drizzle of balsamic vinegar, and tossed with thyme.*

145

MENU · JAPANESE RISOTTO WITH MUSHROOMS AND SCALLIONS ·
MISO-STUFFED EGGPLANT · COLD FRUIT SUSHI WITH
HONEY DIPPING SAUCE · SERVES 4

There are dozens of kinds of miso, each with its own aroma and flavor. All are packed with protein. Whether you use sweet and fine-textured, salty and rough, smooth and tart, or any one of the many other types is strictly a matter of taste. For this menu, however, I strongly advise you use a savory version for the miso broth and a sweet one for the eggplant. As with any risotto, the Japanese Risotto should be served hot. Make the Cold Fruit Sushi first. Squeeze some fresh lemon juice over the pieces, wrap tightly, and refrigerate until it is time to serve dessert.

Japanese Risotto with Mushrooms and Scallions

4½ cups Vegetable Stock (page 13) or
      miso-infused broth
1   tablespoon extra-virgin olive oil
½   cup Kokohu Rose or other short-grain rice
½   cup sake
      Kosher salt and freshly ground black
      pepper
½   cup enoki mushrooms
½   cup chopped scallions
¼   cup Kaiware sprouts

SERVES 4

If using the miso-infused broth, combine 1 tablespoon miso with 4½ cups water and bring to a boil. Reduce the heat and simmer.

In a large saucepan, heat the olive oil over medium-high heat. Add the rice, stirring constantly in one direction, until well coated. Remove the pan from the heat and add the sake. Return to the heat and stir constantly in one direction until all of the liquid is absorbed. Add the stock or broth in ½-cup increments, stirring constantly until the liquid is absorbed with each addition. Season with salt and pepper. Spoon into serving bowls, garnish with the mushrooms, scallions, and sprouts and serve.

OPPOSITE *Risotto with an Asian accent. Japanese rice absorbs sake and chicken stock, achieving the creamy, smooth texture of perfect risotto. Garnish with enoki mushrooms, chopped scallions, and Kaiware sprouts.*

147

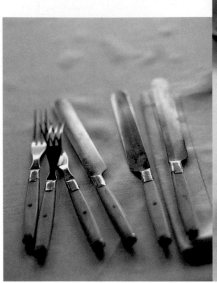

Miso-Stuffed Eggplant

4   *Japanese eggplants, 6 to 8 inches long*

¾   *cup sweet miso*

2   *teaspoons light tamari sauce*

SERVES 4

In a large steamer, steam the eggplant for 10 to 12 minutes, until very tender. Turn on the broiler. Combine the miso and tamari in a small bowl. Make a ½-inch-deep lengthwise slit down the eggplants. Spoon 2 tablespoons of miso into each eggplant. Place on a baking sheet and slide under the broiler until slightly browned, about 2 to 3 minutes.

Cold Fruit Sushi with Honey Dipping Sauce

1   *small honeydew melon*

1   *small cantaloupe*

1   *small pineapple*

2   *tablespoons honey*

SERVES 4

Place the fruit on a cutting board lined with parchment. Trim the tops and bottoms of the melons and pineapple and sit them upright on the cutting board. Using a very sharp knife, cut away the rind, slicing lengthwise, working your way around the fruit. Cut about 24 very thin slices of melon in the same fashion, slicing from top to bottom, allowing the juices to collect on the parchment paper. Slice the pineapple lengthwise into ⅛-inch slices. Pile and cut into matchsticks.

Pour the juices that have collected into a small bowl. Stir in the honey and set aside.

To assemble the fruit sushi, lay the melon slices vertically on the cutting board. Place 3 pineapple matchsticks horizontally at the base of the melon slice and roll. Trim the base so that the rolls sit firmly on a dessert plate. Serve with the honey dipping sauce.

ABOVE *There's a little sushi restaurant, Taka, in Greenwich Village that makes the most fabulous miso-stuffed eggplant that inspired this dish, served on a 1950s teak serving tray.* RIGHT *Spare, cool melon and pineapple prepared sushi-style is a graceful finish to a simple, elegant meal.*

MENU · HALIBUT STEAMED IN GRAPE LEAVES ·
WILTED MUSTARD GREENS · PARSLEY QUINOA SALAD ·
GRAPE COCKTAIL · SERVES 4

Halibut Steamed in Grape Leaves

12	grape leaves, rinsed in water
½	cup coarsely chopped fresh mint
1	tablespoon freshly chopped oregano
1	pound halibut, cut in 4 pieces
	Kosher salt and freshly ground black pepper
1	lemon, very thinly sliced

SERVES 4

Lay 3 grape leaves on the counter with the stem ends intersecting to form a triangle. Sprinkle one quarter of the mint and one quarter of the oregano in the middle of the triangle. Season the fish with salt and pepper and lay on top of the herbs. Lay 2 lemon slices on top of the fish and fold the grape leaves as you would an envelope. Repeat with the remaining fish. Set the fish in the steamer basket and steam 5 to 7 minutes, until the fish is firm to the touch.

Wilted Mustard Greens

2	tablespoons extra-virgin olive oil
1	garlic clove, minced
1	pound mustard greens, washed, rinsed, trimmed, and stems removed
	Kosher salt and freshly ground black pepper

SERVES 4

In a small pan over low heat, combine the oil and garlic and cook until the garlic turns brown and crisp. Do not overcook. Add the mustard greens and cook until wilted and tender, about 3 to 5 minutes. Season with salt and pepper and serve.

Parsley Quinoa Salad

¾	cup quinoa, washed, strained, and rinsed twice
⅓	cup roughly chopped parsley
1	small cucumber, peeled, seeded, and diced
	Juice of ½ lemon
1	teaspoon extra-virgin olive oil
	Kosher salt and freshly ground black pepper

SERVES 4

Combine the quinoa and 1½ cups of water in a 2-quart saucepan over high heat. Bring to a boil, cover, reduce the heat, and simmer 10 to 12 minutes, until all of the water is absorbed. Drain and run under cold water. Toss in the remaining ingredients and serve.

Grape Cocktail

¼	pound green grapes
¼	pound red grapes
¼	pound purple grapes
¼	cup Beaumes de Venise or other dessert wine

SERVES 4

Thoroughly wash and pat dry each bunch of grapes. Divide among 4 dessert plates and serve each with 1 tablespoon of the dessert wine.

This menu is a perfect example of what I call "clean" food. The flavors are clear and straightforward and depend heavily on the quality of the ingredients rather than elaborate techniques. Virtually any firm white-fleshed fish steams beautifully in grape leaves. Grape leaves are only commercially available canned in a very salty brine. Be sure to rinse them before wrapping the fish. The quinoa salad can be made in advance and served at room temperature. The simplest desserts can be the most delicious—the very freshest green, red, and purple grapes become special when set on shaved ice and served with a bit of dessert wine.

ABOVE LEFT *Packaged in briny grape leaves and steamed to moist pefection, halibut is delicately perfumed with fresh herbs and lemon.* **RIGHT** *I love to serve cold grapes on Depression glass dessert plates with these exquisite sterling silver grape scissors.* **OPPOSITE** *The picture of health: Halibut Steamed in Grape Leaves, Parsley Quinoa Salad, and Wilted Mustard Greens.*

MENU · CHARRED EGGPLANT SOUP WITH A RED PEPPER SWIRL · YOGURT-MARINATED SWORDFISH KEBABS · ISRAELI COUSCOUS PILAF · DRIED FRUIT WITH CHOCOLATE DIPPING SAUCE · SERVES 4

This menu was inspired by a trip to Kalustyan's, the oldest and one of the best sources for Middle Eastern, Indian, and Asian ingredients in Manhattan. I love experimenting with the many different grains that they carry. Among my favorites is Israeli Couscous, a medium-grain hand-rolled semolina that is toasted, unlike the much finer grained, more common couscous, which is not toasted. For the soup, I find it easiest to char the eggplants on the stovetop griddle, but you can also roast the eggplants in a high-heated oven until they are fork tender. Charring them gives the soup a deeper smoky flavor. Tangy parsley-speckled yogurt marinade both flavors and tenderizes succulent grilled swordfish. Try to find as many different kinds of dried fruit for dessert—my favorite are dried plums.

Charred Eggplant Soup with a Red Pepper Swirl

2	medium-size eggplants
2	medium-size onions, sliced
4	garlic cloves, minced
2	teaspoons extra-virgin olive oil
4	cups Chicken Stock (page 13) or low-sodium canned
1/4	teaspoon herbes de Provence
1	bay leaf
	Kosher salt and freshly ground black pepper
2	teaspoons fresh lemon juice
1/2	cup buttermilk
1/2	cup Red Pepper Coulis (page 15)
1	tablespoon chopped flat-leaf parsley

SERVES 4

Preheat a cast-iron griddle or skillet over medium-high heat. Place the eggplants on the griddle and char them well, turning from time to time, until the outer skin is burnt and peeling and the inside is very soft, about 15 minutes. Transfer to a bowl and let cool. Trim away the skin and discard. On a parchment-lined cutting board, chop the eggplant and set aside, along with any juice that has accumulated on the parchment.

Meanwhile, combine the onions, garlic, and olive oil in a 3-quart saucepan over medium heat for 5 to 10 minutes, or until they are soft and translucent. Add the chicken stock, herbes de Provence, and bay leaf and bring to a boil. Reduce the heat and simmer for 15 minutes. Season with salt, pepper, and lemon juice. Remove the bay leaf, add the eggplant, and purée the soup in a blender or food processor. Stir in the buttermilk.

Ladle into soup bowls and swirl in the Red Pepper Coulis. Garnish with the parsley and serve.

ABOVE *A Middle Eastern–inspired menu begins with Charred Eggplant Soup with Red Pepper Coulis.* **OPPOSITE** *A succulent swordfish kebab with parsleyed yogurt for dipping and tangy Israeli Couscous Pilaf are ready to eat in less than a half hour.*

153

ABOVE *The stovetop grill is an essential piece of equipment in the Healthy Quick Cook kitchen. Yogurt-Marinated Swordfish Kebabs are grilled to perfection on my double burner grill top.* **OPPOSITE** *A grand ivory ceramic footed serving bowl is bursting with dried plums, pineapples, apricots, bananas, and figs for dipping in glistening chocolate sauce.*

Yogurt-Marinated Swordfish Kebabs

1	pound 1-inch-thick swordfish steaks, rinsed and patted dry, cut into 24 cubes
	Kosher salt and freshly ground black pepper
1	8-ounce container plain nonfat yogurt, 4 tablespoons reserved
2	tablespoons roughly chopped parsley
8	metal skewers
8	red cherry tomatoes
4	yellow cherry tomatoes
4	scallions, halved, then sliced

SERVES 4

Season the fish with salt and pepper. Combine the yogurt and 1 tablespoon parsley in a shallow baking dish and add the fish, turning to coat. Marinate the fish for 15 minutes at room temperature or for 1 hour in the refrigerator.

Meanwhile, combine the reserved yogurt and remaining parsley in a small bowl and mix well.

Thread the skewers, alternating the fish, tomatoes, and scallions, beginning and ending with the scallions.

Prepare a stove-top griddle or outdoor grill. Grill the kebabs 3 to 4 minutes per side, or until opaque. Serve with a dollop of the yogurt sauce.

Israeli Couscous Pilaf

1	tablespoon extra-virgin olive oil
1	medium-size onion, finely chopped
2	cups Israeli couscous
1³⁄₄	cups Chicken Stock (page 13) or low-sodium canned
	Kosher salt and freshly ground black pepper
1	tablespoon lemon juice
2	plum tomatoes, finely diced
1	teaspoon coarsely chopped parsley

SERVES 4

In a saucepan over medium heat, place 1 teaspoon of olive oil and sauté the onion until translucent. Add the couscous and stir until coated and slightly golden, about 1 minute. Add the chicken stock to cover, then cover and simmer until the liquid is absorbed, about 10 to 15 minutes. Season with salt and pepper. Add the lemon juice, tomatoes, and parsley and serve.

Dried Fruit with Chocolate Dipping Sauce

2	tablespoons Dutch cocoa
2	tablespoons sugar
¹⁄₂	cup nonfat sweetened condensed milk
¹⁄₂–³⁄₄	pound mixed dried fruit (apricots, plums, pineapples, bananas, pears, papaya, mango)

SERVES 4

In a small bowl, combine the cocoa, sugar, and 2 tablespoons of water, and stir until smooth. In a small saucepan over medium-high heat, combine the milk and cocoa mixture and bring to a boil, stirring constantly, about 1 to 2 minutes. Pour into a serving bowl and pass with the dried fruit.

MENU · RUSTIC GRUYÈRE CROUTONS · SEVEN-ONION SOUP · CURLY ENDIVE WITH CITRUS VINAIGRETTE · PRUNES POACHED IN ARMAGNAC WITH ENLIGHTENED CRÈME FRAÎCHE · SERVES 4

I love French onion soup, but the long cooking time and gobs of cheese characteristic of the classic version no longer appeal to me. My version—deconstructed, if you will—achieves the same full flavor of the traditional soup from dried porcini mushrooms and a bit of marsala wine. The croutons need only thin shavings of assertively flavored cheese to satisfy. I use Gruyère, but Emmental and Beaufort are excellent, too.

Rustic Gruyère Croutons

½   small loaf whole-grain bread, broken into
      4 rough pieces
2   ounces Gruyère cheese, shaved into
      paper-thin slices
      Kosher salt and freshly ground black
      pepper

MAKES 4 CROUTONS

Toast the bread on both sides. Top each piece of bread with a slice of Gruyère and slide under the broiler until the cheese bubbles. Season with salt and pepper and serve.

Seven-Onion Soup

2   tablespoons extra-virgin olive oil
2   red onions, coarsely chopped
2   white onions, coarsely chopped
2   yellow onions, coarsely chopped
12   fresh pearl onions or 10 ounces frozen
3   shallots, coarsely chopped
2   leeks, washed and cut into ¼-inch rings
4   medium bunches of chives, coarsely
      chopped
¼   cup marsala wine
6   cups Beef Stock (page 14) or
      low-sodium canned
2   tablespoons coarsely chopped dried
      porcini
1   tablespoon fresh thyme leaves, plus 4
      sprigs of thyme

SERVES 4

In a 4-quart soup pot over medium heat, combine the olive oil, red, white, yellow, and pearl onions, and the shallots and sauté until golden brown and soft. Add the leeks and chives and cook until the onions turn a deep golden brown, about 5 minutes. Add the wine and cook, stirring, 2 minutes more, or until the mixture begins to bubble. Add 2 cups of stock every 15 minutes for the next 45 minutes, allowing the liquid to reduce by one fourth after each addition. Add the mushrooms and thyme leaves with the last 2 cups of stock. The soup will be a very deep brown. Ladle into deep soup bowls and garnish with the thyme sprigs.

Curly Endive with Citrus Vinaigrette

1   large head of curly endive, washed,
      dried, and torn into bite-size pieces
¾   cup Citrus Vinaigrette (page 17)
      Kosher salt and freshly ground black
      pepper

SERVES 4

In a large salad bowl, place the endive. Drizzle the vinaigrette over the greens and toss to coat. Season to taste with salt and pepper.

OPPOSITE *Seven-Onion Soup with Rustic Gruyère Croutons is as flavorful as classic French onion soup—without all the fat.* **LEFT** *While not traditional, I eat lacy-edged curly endive with the onion soup—not before or after.*

Prunes Poached in Armagnac with Enlightened Crème Fraîche

16	*pitted prunes*
1/4	*cup dried cranberries*
1½	*cups cranberry juice*
2	*tablespoons Armagnac or orange juice*
2	*tablespoons sugar*
1/2	*cup Enlightened Crème Fraîche (page 14)*

In a large saucepan over medium heat, combine all of the ingredients except the Enlightened Crème Fraîche and cook, stirring occasionally, until the sauce is thick enough to coat the back of a spoon, about 15 minutes. Spoon 4 prunes and some of the sauce onto each of 4 dessert plates and drizzle 2 teaspoons of Enlightened Crème Fraîche over each.

ABOVE *The blue-gray hue of my ironstone soup terrine showcases beautifully the rich mahogany broth in Seven Onion Soup.* **RIGHT** *Poaching prunes, or most any whole fruit—pears, apricots, or bananas—is foolproof.*

MENU · ROAST PHEASANT WITH GRAPES AND WALNUTS · ROASTED PARSNIPS AND ONIONS · RICE PUDDING · SERVES 4

Pheasant is delicious roasted, so long as the game bird is very young. When asking your butcher for pheasant, request a young female, since their flesh is juicier than older pheasants. As easy to roast as turkey or chicken, pheasant is somewhat less fatty and, if not farm-raised, far more flavorful than commercial poultry. I love the combination of parsnips and cipollines. Also referred to as wild onions, fresh cipollines are the bittersweet bulbs of the grape hyacinth, and are available for a short time in the fall. If you can't find them, use some other sweet onion, such as Vidalias, cutting them into walnut-size pieces. My version of rice pudding is made on the stovetop, and is essentially a sweet risotto. Add as much warm milk as you like during the final cooking stages to achieve a consistency you like.

Roast Pheasant with Grapes and Walnuts

1	4-pound pheasant, washed and patted dry
1	tablespoon extra-virgin olive oil
	Kosher salt and freshly ground black pepper
1/2	cup mixed fresh herbs such as rosemary, thyme, savory, and basil
1	lemon, quartered
8	cipolline onions
1	cup Chicken Stock (page 13) or low-sodium canned
1/2	cup marsala wine
1	cup mixed green and red grapes
1/2	cup coarsely chopped walnuts
8	large radicchio leaves

SERVES 4

Preheat the oven to 425°F.

Rub the pheasant with the olive oil. Season with salt and pepper. Stuff with fresh herbs and the lemon and truss. Spread the onions in a roasting pan and lay the pheasant on top of them. Add the chicken stock and marsala wine to the pan. Roast 35 to 45 minutes, or until the thigh juices run clear when pricked with a fork, basting every 15 to 20 minutes with the pan juices. If the feet of the pheasant begin to darken, tent with foil. Transfer to a cutting board and let rest. Meanwhile, transfer the roasting pan to the stovetop, skim the fat, and bring the pan juices to a boil, scraping any browned bits from the pan. Add the grapes and walnuts and cook 15 minutes, or until the grapes are soft and the juices are thickened. Crush some of the grapes with the back of a spoon to release their juices. Slice the pheasant into ¼-inch slices and serve over the radicchio. Spoon the grapes and walnuts alongside and season with salt and pepper.

OPPOSITE *Drabware plates and molded ivory handled flatware set the autumnal tone for a lovely—and light—dinner of Roast Pheasant with Grapes and Walnuts, cradled in beautiful radicchio leaves.*

Roasted Parsnips and Onions

1	pound parsnips, ends trimmed
1	pound cipolline onions, peeled
1/4	cup fresh rosemary
2	tablespoons extra-virgin olive oil

SERVES 4

Preheat the oven to 425°F.

In a roasting pan, combine the parsnips, onions, and rosemary. Add the olive oil and toss until the vegetables are thoroughly coated. Roast for 40 to 45 minutes, shaking the pan every 15 minutes, until the vegetables are deep amber.

Rice Pudding

5	cups skim milk
1/2	teaspoon pure vanilla extract
1/3	cup granulated sugar
1/4	teaspoon cinnamon
	Pinch of freshly ground nutmeg
1	teaspoon butter
1/2	cup Arborio rice
1/4	cup Champagne or white grape juice
1	tablespoon Demerara sugar or raw sugar

SERVES 4

In a saucepan, combine the milk, vanilla, sugar, cinnamon, and nutmeg and heat over medium heat until the sugar is dissolved. Turn the heat to low to keep the mixture warm. In a large saucepan, melt the butter. Add the rice and stir to coat. Add the Champagne and cook, stirring until the liquid is absorbed. Ladle the milk into the rice ½ cup at a time, stirring with each new addition, about 35 minutes. Remove from the stove and stir in the remaining milk, if desired, to achieve a creamier consistency. Divide among dessert bowls and sprinkle with the Demerara sugar.

ABOVE *The flavor of golden roasted whole parsnips and cipolline onions is enhanced by fragrant rosemary.* **OPPOSITE** *Whenever I make rice pudding, served here in footed ironstone egg cups, I am reminded of my mother's version—it filled the entire house with the tantalizing aroma of cinnamon and nutmeg.*

MENU · CRUNCHY SPROUT AND DAIKON SALAD WITH MINT ·
SPICE-RUBBED ROAST PORK LOIN ·
SEARED PLUMS · THIN LEMON TART · SERVES 4

This menu is perfectly suited to entertaining or a special family celebration. Trussing the pork loin prevents the herbs from shifting during cooking. What's more, it makes a beautiful presentation. Seared fruits are simple, healthful accompaniments to roasted meats; use slightly overripe fruit. The lemon tarts are so delicious that I can't imagine ever giving them up entirely. Don't be put off by the amount of butter in the pastry dough. It is rolled very thin and the serving is just enough to satisfy any sweet craving. I love to drink a cup of Earl Grey tea with my tart.

Crunchy Sprout and Daikon Salad with Mint

1	cup shredded purple cabbage
1	cup shredded green cabbage
1/2	cup shredded daikon radish
2	cups shredded carrots
1	cup sunflower sprouts
1	cup pea shoots
2	tablespoons mint leaves
4	tablespoons Sesame Vinaigrette (page 17)

SERVES 4

In a large salad bowl, combine all of the ingredients except the vinaigrette and toss thoroughly. Drizzle the Sesame Vinaigrette over and toss to coat the vegetables thoroughly.

Spice-Rubbed Roast Pork Loin

4	tablespoons celery seed
2	tablespoons very coarsely ground caraway seeds
2	8-ounce pork tenderloins, trimmed of fat
3	tablespoons Dijon mustard
	Kosher salt and freshly ground black pepper
2	large sprigs of sage
	Kitchen string
1	tablespoon extra-virgin olive oil
	Seared Plums (page 167)

SERVES 4

Preheat the oven to 400°F.

Combine the celery seed and caraway seeds on a shallow plate and set aside. Brush the tenderloins with mustard all over. Season with salt and pepper and roll into the spice mix. Lay a sage sprig on each loin and truss every inch. In an ovenproof skillet over high heat, add the olive oil. Sear the loins on one side for about 1 minute. Turn the pork and place in the oven. Roast for about 7 to 9 minutes; turn and roast for 7 to 9 minutes more. The tenderloin will be medium when the internal temperature, taken with a meat thermometer, is 145°F. for medium, 150°F. for medium well. Remove the meat to a cutting board and let rest for 10 minutes. Cut into 1/2-inch slices. Arrange 3 slices on each plate and serve with the Seared Plums.

ABOVE *Pan juices from the spiced pork loin are spooned over the plate before arranging thin slices with brilliant red roasted plums.*
OPPOSITE *I use a French mandoline to create perfect shreds of purple and green cabbages, daikon radishes, and carrots for Crunchy Sprout and Daikon Salad with Mint.*

Seared Plums

4	plums, cut into ½-inch wedges
6	sprigs of thyme
2	tablespoons balsamic vinegar
1½	teaspoons honey
½	teaspoon kosher salt
1	teaspoon freshly ground black pepper

SERVES 4

Preheat the oven to 400°F.

In a bowl, combine all of the ingredients and set aside for 10 minutes.

Heat a nonstick ovenproof skillet over medium heat, add the plum mixture, and cook 30 seconds to 1 minute, until the surface of the plums are seared and caramel-colored.

Transfer the plums to the oven and bake for about 10 minutes, or until the plum skins are just beginning to break and the color is vibrant.

Thin Lemon Tart

½	cup all-purpose flour
½	cup plus 1 teaspoon sugar
½	teaspoon grated lemon zest
	Pinch of kosher salt
3½	tablespoons chilled unsalted butter, cut into pieces
3	teaspoons ice water
4	large, very thin slices lemon

In a bowl, combine the flour, 1 teaspoon sugar, lemon zest, and salt. With a fork, blend in the butter until the mixture resembles coarse meal. Add 2 teaspoons of ice water and toss until incorporated. Add remaining ice water, tossing with a fork until the mixture begins to come together. Form the dough into a ball, wrap in plastic wrap, and chill for 30 minutes.

Preheat the oven to 350°F. On a lightly floured surface with a floured rolling pin, roll out the dough into a 7 × 4-inch rectangle. Transfer the dough to a baking sheet and poke it all over with a fork. Bake until golden, about 10 minutes. Transfer to a cooling rack set over a baking sheet lined with parchment paper.

Meanwhile, in a small saucepan, stir together 2 tablespoons water and remaining ½ cup sugar. Bring the mixture to a boil over moderately high heat, brushing down the sides of the pan with a pastry brush dipped in water. Turn the heat to low and simmer for 10 minutes, or until the caramel is a light amber.

Arrange the lemon slices down the center of the pastry and pour the hot caramel over the lemon slices. Let the pastry cool. Using a very sharp knife, cut into 4 pieces and serve.

ABOVE LEFT *Quickly seared then roasted in the oven, fleshy, sweet plums are showered with thyme for a savory side dish.* **ABOVE RIGHT** *Super thin, super lemony and just sweet enough, a small piece of a Thin Lemon Tart satisfies my occasional sweet tooth.* **OPPOSITE** *Rolled in celery and caraway seeds, seasoned with sage, and trussed with string, pork tenderloins are ready for a quick sear in the skillet.*

MENU · BUTTERNUT SQUASH SOUP WITH ROASTED GARLIC · SEARED BEEF AND ORANGES WITH ARUGULA · BROILED STAR FRUIT IN GINGERED BROTH · SERVES 4

Pretty, elegant and ready to serve in little more than an hour, this menu is perfect for casual fall entertaining. While the squash and garlic are roasting for the soup, prepare the broth for the dessert, and while it simmers, marinate the beef for the entrée. To save time and unnecessary work, ask your butcher to cut the tenderloin into tournedos for you. I like to serve toasted slices of rustic bread slathered with roasted garlic with the soup course when I entertain for a more substantial meal.

Butternut Squash Soup with Roasted Garlic

1   large butternut squash, halved and
    seeded

Kosher salt and freshly ground black
    pepper

4   sprigs of fresh thyme

4   large Roasted Garlic (page 14) cloves

1   cup warm Chicken Stock (page 13) or
    low-sodium canned

SERVES 4

Preheat the oven to 425°F. Line a baking sheet with parchment paper.

Season the squash with salt and pepper and tuck 2 sprigs of thyme into each cavity. Place, cut side down, on the baking sheet and roast until fork-tender, about 40 minutes. When the squash is cool enough to handle, discard the thyme; peel the squash and coarsely chop. Combine the squash, garlic, and ½ cup of the chicken stock in a food processor and purée until smooth. Add the remaining stock gradually until the mixture forms a very loose purée. Season the soup with salt and pepper.

ABOVE LEFT *Remove the papery skin from garlic roasted to sweet perfection, and spread the smooth, candied cloves on lightly toasted bread.* **ABOVE RIGHT** *When roasting butternut squash and garlic, I use a parchment-lined baking tray for easy cleanup.* **OPPOSITE** *Minton patterned brown transferware dinner plates, molded ivory handled flatware, and pumpkin napkins arranged on a ivory linen tablecloth set the tone for an autumnal meal.*

169

ABOVE *I arrange succulent seared beef tenderloin, peppery arugula, and juicy oranges so they are slightly overlapping, but tossed together as in a composed salad and dressed with the pan juices would be perfect for lunch.* **OPPOSITE** *Carambola, commonly known as star fruit, is among my favorite fruits. I love to eat them thinly sliced and raw, but a fall chill inspired me to broil then bathe them in a gentle gingered broth.*

Seared Beef and Oranges with Arugula

1	pound beef tenderloin, trimmed of fat and sliced into 4 1-inch-thick tournedos
	Kosher salt and freshly ground black pepper
2	tablespoons low-sodium soy sauce
1	teaspoon grated ginger
1	garlic clove, minced
2	tablespoons rice vinegar
3	oranges, 2 peeled, pithed, and sliced into 6 rings, plus 1 for juicing
1/4	teaspoon extra-virgin olive oil
1	large bunch of arugula (about 1/2 pound), trimmed and rinsed

SERVES 4

Season the beef with salt and pepper. Combine the soy sauce, ginger, garlic, 1 tablespoon rice vinegar, and 1 tablespoon orange juice in a shallow dish. Add the beef, turn to coat, and marinate at room temperature for 15 minutes. Meanwhile, rub the olive oil into a cast-iron skillet and place over high heat. When the skillet is heated through, place the beef in the skillet and sear for 2 minutes per side. Remove to a cutting board to rest for 5 minutes.

Place the orange slices in the pan in batches and sear for 30 seconds on each side. Remove to a plate.

Meanwhile, in a large bowl, whisk together the remaining orange juice and vinegar and salt and pepper. Add the arugula and toss to coat.

Slice the beef tournedos into 1/2-inch-thick slices. To serve, place a handful of arugula on each of 4 plates, arrange 3 orange slices over the arugula, and top with sliced beef. Season with freshly ground pepper and serve.

Broiled Star Fruit in Gingered Broth

1	3-inch piece of fresh ginger, peeled and cut into 1/4-inch slices
1/2	cinnamon stick
2	whole cloves
10	coriander seeds
1	tablespoon honey
2	star fruit, ends trimmed and each sliced into 8 stars
1	tablespoon brown sugar

SERVES 4

In a 2-quart saucepan, combine 4 cups of water with the ginger, cinnamon, cloves, and coriander and bring to a boil. Reduce the heat and simmer 30 minutes. Add the honey and stir to dissolve. Strain and allow to cool. Meanwhile, place a broiler rack about 6 inches from the heat source. Place the star fruit on a baking sheet and sprinkle 1 tablespoon brown sugar over the top. Broil until the sugar bubbles and begins to brown. Place 4 stars in each of 4 shallow bowls, ladle the gingered broth into each, and serve.

WINTER

Winter's menus are filled with recipes reminiscent of the old-fashioned comfort foods we all know and love from childhood. A pot-au-feu, a ragout, a burger, and even pork chops; these fill our minds with feelings of great dining and utter satisfaction. The traditional versions of these foods are often saturated with fat, covered with rich sauces, and served with noodles, bread, or rice; they fit into categories very unlike "lite" and "low calorie." However, we've worked hard to make the tuna burger delicious and healthy, the ragout extremely low fat (only one tablespoon of olive oil), and the chicken soup very high protein. We like to use the oven in winter, for roasting fish, meats, and vegetables, for braising meats, and for baking desserts. We use the stovetop for steaming, boiling, and pan searing—all quick methods to retain the most flavor possible and as much of the nutritional value of the foods as well. Winter foods can be even more strongly flavored than those of autumn, and reliance on spices and herbs is tantamount to excellent results: fennel, cinnamon, thyme, cranberries, sage, radicchio, and even wasabi (Japanese horseradish) all contribute to the exotic, delicious dishes in the menus that follow. Winter's desserts are extremely tasty—delightful combinations of unusual flavors, including pears and cranberries, ginger and pears, green tea, and rosé wine with winter blackberries.

MENU · POT-AU-FEU ·
HORSERADISH WHIPPED POTATOES ·
CLEMENTINES WITH CRACKED BLACK PEPPER · SERVES 4

I love the way Pot-au-Feu fills the kitchen with the unmistakable aroma of simmering root vegetables. Almost any combination of meat and vegetables can be used. I always use lean, flavorful cuts of meat and vegetables such as carrots and parsnips that make the broth extra sweet. This dish also makes the perfect leftover lunch or snack. Spoon the horseradish-spiked whipped potatoes right into each bowl of Pot-au-Feu so that they soak up every bit of broth.

Pot-au-Feu

1	*pound beef tenderloin, trimmed of fat and cut into ¼-inch-thick slices*
6	*cups Chicken Stock (page 13) or low-sodium canned*
2	*medium carrots, peeled, sliced crosswise ½ inch thick on the diagonal, and quartered*
1	*small rutabaga (about 1 pound), peeled, sliced crosswise ½ inch thick on the diagonal, and quartered*
2	*parsnips, pared, sliced crosswise ½ inch thick on a diagonal, and quartered*
1	*large leek, white part only, quartered*
2	*celery stalks, peeled, sliced crosswise ½ inch thick on the diagonal, and quartered*
	Kosher salt and freshly ground black pepper
1	*sprig of fresh thyme*
1	*sprig of fresh rosemary*
1	*sprig of fresh parsley*

SERVES 4

In a large, heavy stockpot over medium heat, brown the meat. Add the chicken stock, vegetables, and herbs and bring to a simmer, about 20 to 30 minutes, until the vegetables are fork-tender. Raise the heat if necessary to maintain the simmer. Using a slotted spoon, remove the meat to a cutting board. Spoon the vegetables among 4 large shallow bowls. Ladle some broth into each bowl. Slice the meat into 8 slices and spoon 2 slices into each bowl.

ABOVE *Fresh grated horseradish is a must for the Horseradish Whipped Potatoes.* **OPPOSITE** *The cold months are perfect for Pot-au-Feu, which translated in French means "pot on fire."*

Horseradish Whipped Potatoes

2   large russet potatoes, peeled and cut
       into 1-inch cubes
1/3 cup skim milk, heated
2   teaspoons extra-virgin olive oil
1½ teaspoons prepared horseradish
       Kosher salt and freshly ground black
       pepper

SERVES 4

In a 2-quart saucepan, cover the potatoes with cold water and bring to a boil. Reduce the heat and simmer 15 minutes, or until fork-tender. Drain and transfer the potatoes to a bowl. Using a large fork, mash the potatoes together with the remaining ingredients until light, about 2 minutes.

Clementines with Cracked Black Pepper

4   very sweet and juicy clementines
       Freshly cracked black peppercorns, for
       sprinkling

SERVES 4

Place the clementines on a small plate and pass, along with a small dish of cracked black peppercorns. Serve with café au lait.

LEFT *I serve the entire meal—Pot-au-Feu and Horseradish Whipped Potatoes—in Wedgwood yellowware rimmed soup bowls. I love to eat the potatoes with a spoon so that I can scoop up a bit of broth with every bite.* **ABOVE** *When the weather becomes cold, turn to citrus for dessert. I like clementines sprinkled with a little black pepper between sips of café au lait from my French stencilware paneled bowl. I keep this Old Paris porcelain compote full of clementines when they're in season.*

MENU · ROASTED MONKFISH ·
CHUNKY CIPOLLINE TOMATO COMPOTE ·
FENNEL CARPACCIO WITH BLOOD ORANGES AND
BLACK OLIVES · MOCHA POT DE CRÈME · SERVES 4

Fennel tastes best thinly sliced. I love to serve it this way, arranged flat on a plate and topped with a savory mix of blood oranges and just a few oil-cured olives, roughly chopped to give the illusion of volume. Moderately firm-textured monkfish is just sturdy enough to stand up to a very hot oven. Other fish, such as mahimahi, halibut, and grouper, can be used here. Despite its incredibly decadent taste and appearance, the Mocha Pot de Crème is low in fat.

ABOVE *Whisper-thin fennel, juicy blood oranges, and savory black olives are tossed and dressed with the collected juice from the oranges.* **OPPOSITE** *Roasted Monkfish set on a bed of Chunky Cipolline Tomato Compote is breathtaking in a hand-decorated pearlware Wedgwood rimmed soup bowl. I serve this with my hollow-handled fish forks and knives when I'm entertaining.*

Roasted Monkfish

1	tablespoon extra-virgin olive oil
1½	pounds monkfish, cut into 4 pieces
¼	cup dry white wine or dry vermouth
2	cups Chunky Cipolline Tomato Compote (page 180)
	Kosher salt and freshly ground black pepper

SERVES 4

Preheat the oven to 450°F.

Heat the oil in a skillet over high heat until hot but not smoking. Add the monkfish, shaking the pan as you add the fish to prevent sticking. Sear the fish on one side until golden brown, about 2 to 3 minutes. Transfer to the oven and roast until opaque and firm to the touch, about 8 minutes.

Transfer the fish to a warm plate and set aside. Place the skillet over medium heat and add the wine or vermouth and ¼ cup water, scraping the browned bits from the pan. Add the Chunky Cipolline Tomato Compote to the skillet and cook until heated through. Season to taste with salt and pepper. Spoon the compote among 4 dinner plates, arrange a piece of the monkfish over the compote, and serve.

Chunky Cipolline Tomato Compote

1   tablespoon extra-virgin olive oil
20 pearl onions, peeled
    Kosher salt and freshly ground black
      pepper
1   14-ounce can whole peeled tomatoes,
      seeded and chopped, juices reserved
1   cup white wine
1   teaspoon balsamic vinegar
½   cup loosely packed basil, washed

MAKES 2 CUPS

In a large, ovenproof skillet, heat the olive oil over medium heat. Add the onions and salt and pepper and cook until the onions are soft and golden, about 8 to 10 minutes. Add the tomato juice, wine, and vinegar and bring to a boil. Reduce the heat to low and simmer until the onions are tender and begin to separate, about 15 minutes. Stir in the tomatoes and cook 5 minutes more. Stir in the basil. Transfer to a bowl and cover to keep warm. The compote will keep, tightly covered, in the refrigerator for 3 days.

OPPOSITE *Cold winter nights call for warm desserts, warm chocolate desserts like rich Mocha Pot de Crème, which I serve in sweet Wedgwood porcelain teacups.*

Fennel Carpaccio with Blood Oranges and Black Olives

2   blood oranges
1   medium-size fennel bulb, stalks removed
      and very thinly sliced, preferably
      with a mandoline or vegetable slicer
12 oil-cured black olives, pitted and
      quartered
    Kosher salt and freshly ground black
      pepper

SERVES 4

Over a bowl, cut the peel and pith from the oranges and cut the sections free from the membranes. Squeeze the membranes over the orange sections, then discard. Divide the fennel, orange sections, and olives among 4 salad plates. Drizzle the juice from the oranges over the salad and season with salt and pepper.

Mocha Pot de Crème

¼   cup Dutch-process cocoa powder,
      sifted
½   cup plus 1 tablespoon skim milk
¼   cup low-fat evaporated milk
1   large egg
1   large egg white
¾   cup granulated sugar
    Pinch of kosher salt
    Confectioners' sugar, for sprinkling

SERVES 4

Preheat the oven to 325°F. Line a shallow baking pan with a cloth towel and set aside.

Place the cocoa powder in a mixing bowl. In another bowl, combine the skim milk and the evaporated milk. Slowly whisk about 3 tablespoons of the milk mixture into the cocoa powder until it forms a thick paste. Whisk in the remaining milk mixture until thoroughly combined and set aside.

In a large bowl, combine the egg, egg white, granulated sugar, and salt and whisk together until thoroughly combined. Whisk in the cocoa-milk mixture until thoroughly combined. Divide the mixture among four 4-ounce ovenproof demitasse cups and place in the prepared baking pan; fill the baking pan halfway with water. Transfer to the oven and bake until the puddings are set when lightly jiggled, about 50 minutes. Remove the puddings from the water bath, transfer to a wire rack, and let cool 20 to 30 minutes. Dust the puddings with confectioners' sugar and serve warm.

MENU · ROASTED WHOLE SNAPPER · HARICOTS VERTS · SPLIT OVEN-ROASTED POTATOES · PEAR CRANBERRY CRISP · SERVES 4

I love everything roasted—fish, potatoes, vegetables—everything. It is an excellent low-fat cooking technique because very little added fat is necessary to carry the flavor of the food. High heat concentrates and seals in food's natural flavor—two jobs that only a few other techniques can do without the help of butter, oil, or other fatty transporter of flavor. A hot oven and a good heavy-bottomed roasting pan or skillet are essential. The pear and cranberry crisp has a traditional topping—it is simply spooned sparingly over the fruit.

Roasted Whole Snapper

1	*fennel bulb, with fronds attached*
4	*small white onions, peeled*
2	*lemons, quartered*
1	*cup good-quality white wine*
1	*whole snapper (about 1½ pounds)*
1	*tablespoon extra-virgin olive oil*
	Kosher salt and freshly ground black pepper
3	*sprigs of fresh dill*
3	*sprigs of fresh parsley*

SERVES 4

Preheat the oven to 425°F.

In a heavy roasting pan or large cast-iron skillet, toss together the fennel, onions, 5 lemon quarters, and the wine. Rub the snapper all over with olive oil and season inside and out with salt and pepper. Stuff the cavity with the herbs and the remaining lemons. Roast about 30 minutes (15 minutes for each inch of thickness), until the flesh just begins to flake.

Haricots Verts

1	*pound haricots verts, stem ends removed*
	Kosher salt
3	*tablespoons fresh lemon juice*

SERVES 4

Prepare a large bowl of ice water and set aside. Bring a 4-quart pot of lightly salted water to a rolling boil. Add the haricots verts and blanch until vibrant, about 5 minutes. Drain in a colander, then submerge in the bowl of ice water. Drain and arrange in a serving bowl. Add salt and lemon juice, toss, and serve family style.

OPPOSITE *A whole snapper fits perfectly in my elongated French copper roasting pan. Set on a bed of small white onions and perfumed with dill and parsley, snapper served whole is dramatic. Haricot verts are blanched and tossed in lemon juice for a simple accompaniment.*

183

Split Oven-Roasted Potatoes

2   *baking potatoes, scrubbed and halved lengthwise*

1   *tablespoon extra-virgin olive oil*
    Kosher salt

2   *tablespoons coarsely chopped fresh chives*

SERVES 4

Preheat the oven to 450°F.

Place the potatoes skin side down in a roasting pan and roast for 35 minutes, or until the potatoes have a golden brown crust. Arrange on a serving platter, drizzle with the oil, and sprinkle with salt and the chives.

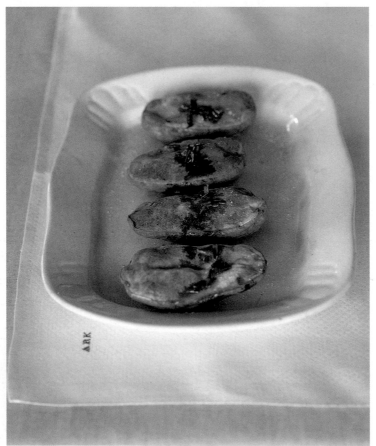

Pear Cranberry Crisp

3   *very ripe pears, peeled, cored, and cut into chunks*

1   *cup whole cranberries*

¼   *cup maple syrup*

2   *tablespoons lemon juice*

½   *cup oatmeal*

¼   *cup brown sugar*

1   *tablespoon flour*

1   *tablespoon butter*

½   *cup Enlightened Crème Fraîche (page 14) or vanilla frozen yogurt*

SERVES 4

Preheat the oven to 400°F.

In a medium bowl, combine the pears, cranberries, maple syrup, and lemon juice and toss. Set aside. In another bowl, combine the oatmeal, brown sugar, and flour. Cut in the butter until the consistency resembles coarse crumbs and the dough just barely holds together. Spoon the cranberry mixture into an 8 × 8-inch baking dish and spoon the dry mixture over it. Bake for 10 minutes, or until the topping is brown and crisp. Reduce the heat to 350°F. and bake for 20 to 25 minutes more, or until the fruit is bubbling. Serve with Enlightened Crème Fraîche or vanilla frozen yogurt.

LEFT *Only the best-quality olive oil is used on these baked potatoes.* **RIGHT** *Bursting with pears and cranberries, my rosy winter crisp is stunning on painted Limoges gilt-rimmed dessert plates.*

MENU · MIXED CHICORIES WITH WARM APPLE THYME DRESSING · THE VERY BEST CHICKEN SOUP · CRUSTY SOURDOUGH BREAD WITH PARSLEY PESTO · CINNAMON CHOCOLATE FROZEN YOGURT SANDWICHES · SERVES 4

This soup and salad menu is perfect for a wintry afternoon lunch or early-evening dinner. I often double the soup recipe and reheat it for lunch the next day. Chicories tend to be strong and bitter tasting. You typically find them sautéed or wilted, but I like to eat them raw, tossed with a warm, slightly sweet vinaigrette and crisp apples. Pesto's fatty reputation—pine nuts are loaded with fat—is changed easily by increasing the proportion of herbs to oil and adding a clove or two of roasted garlic for a flavor boost.

Mixed Chicories with Warm Apple Thyme Dressing

4   tablespoons *Warm Apple Thyme Dressing (page 15)*
1   *pound mixed chicories (endive, radicchio, curly endive, frisée, dandelion), trimmed and washed*
    Freshly ground black pepper

SERVES 4

Place the dressing in a large bowl. Add the chicories and toss to coat. Season with pepper and serve.

The Very Best Chicken Soup

8   *cups Chicken Stock (page 13) or low-sodium canned*
2   *8-ounce skinless, boneless chicken breasts, trimmed of fat*
2   *large carrots, sliced into 1/4-inch rounds (about 2 1/2 cups)*
1   *small fennel bulb, sliced very thin, preferably on a mandoline*
1/2 *cup puntarella or other bitter greens, such as escarole*
1   *cup cooked cranberry, white, navy, or Great Northern beans*
    Kosher salt and freshly ground black pepper

SERVES 4

In a 3-quart soup pot, simmer the stock. Add the chicken and poach until opaque and firm, about 10 minutes. Transfer to a plate. Add the carrots to the broth and cook until fork-tender, about 10 minutes. Add the fennel, greens, and beans and simmer. Shred the chicken into 1-inch strips with your hands. Add to the pot and simmer until the chicken is heated through, about 2 minutes. Season with salt and pepper. Ladle into 4 shallow soup bowls and serve.

LEFT *Sweet Apple Thyme Dressing balances the sharp bite of chicory and radicchio.* **RIGHT** *My version of chicken soup is brimming with healthful beans, carrots, and bitter greens.*

Cinnamon Chocolate Frozen Yogurt Sandwiches

$1/2$	cup Dutch-process cocoa
$1/2$	cup all-purpose flour
$3/4$	teaspoon cinnamon
$1/4$	teaspoon salt
2	tablespoons unsalted butter, softened
$1/4$	cup dark brown sugar
$1/4$	cup granulated sugar
$1/2$	teaspoon pure vanilla extract
1	large egg white
$1/2$	pint nonfat frozen vanilla yogurt

MAKES 2 DOZEN COOKIES
(12 SANDWICHES)

Preheat the oven to 350°F. Line 2 baking sheets with parchment.

In a large bowl, sift together the cocoa, flour, cinnamon, and salt and set aside. In the bowl of an electric mixer, combine the butter, sugars, and vanilla. Beat on medium speed for 3 to 5 minutes until light and fluffy. Add the egg white and combine well. Add the flour mixture and mix until just combined. Form into a ball, cover tightly with plastic wrap, and refrigerate for 15 to 20 minutes. Using a melon baller or teaspoon, scoop the dough and drop onto the baking sheet. Flatten gently with the palm of your hand. Bake for 10 to 12 minutes and remove to a cooling rack.

When cool, spoon about a tablespoon of frozen yogurt on the flat side of the cookie and top with a second cookie. Serve. The prepared sandwiches can be stored in a rigid container and frozen up to 1 week.

ABOVE *Generously spread my slimmed-down Parsley Pesto onto crusty sourdough or swirl it into the chicken soup.* **OPPOSITE** *What's for dessert? A dramatic stack of silver-dollar-sized Cinnamon Chocolate Frozen Yogurt Sandwiches, pulled straight from the freezer and set on a Wedgwood drabware plate.*

Crusty Sourdough Bread with Parsley Pesto

1	large bunch of flat-leaf parsley (about 1 packed cup)
2	tablespoons extra-virgin olive oil
1	small garlic clove, minced
2	teaspoons lime juice
	Kosher salt and freshly ground black pepper
4	thick slices sourdough bread, grilled or toasted

SERVES 4

In a small bowl, combine all of the ingredients except the bread and mash together with a fork. Serve with the bread slices.

MENU · TURKEY MEATBALL SOUP WITH ESCAROLE AND
PAPPARDELLE · CHOCOLATE SORBET · SERVES 4

I devised this recipe for meatballs because, while I refrain from eating the beef version bound with egg yolks and bread crumbs, I really missed making them. Whenever possible, make your own stock—to my mind it tastes far better than the canned version. The beauty of soups like this one is that they can provide most of the nutrition you need in one bowl. What's more, you can control the proportions easily—add more greens than pasta and toss in just a meatball or two for a healthy, satisfying dinner in no time.

Turkey Meatball Soup with Escarole and Pappardelle

1	pound ground turkey
1	egg white
1	cup coarsely chopped parsley leaves
1	medium-size onion, coarsely chopped
2	garlic cloves, minced
1	teaspoon kosher salt, plus more to taste
1/4	teaspoon freshly cracked black pepper, plus more to taste
1	teaspoon extra-virgin olive oil
3	shallots, minced
8	cups Chicken Stock (page 13) or low-sodium canned
1	tablespoon thyme
4	ounces pappardelle, cooked al dente
1	bunch escarole (about 3/4 pound), trimmed, washed, and coarsely chopped

SERVES 4

In a bowl, combine the turkey, egg white, parsley, onion, half of the garlic, salt, and pepper and fluff with a fork. Shape into balls the size of walnuts (about 24 meatballs). In a large nonstick skillet over medium heat, cook the meatballs until cooked through, crispy, and golden, about 5 minutes. Using a slotted spoon, transfer the meatballs to a paper towel–lined plate.

In a soup pot over medium-high heat, add the oil, remaining garlic, and shallots and cook until translucent and soft, about 5 minutes. Add the chicken stock and simmer. Add the thyme, meatballs, and pasta and return to a simmer. Stir in the escarole and salt and pepper to taste. Ladle into 4 deep soup bowls and serve.

ABOVE *I always serve my Turkey Meatball Soup with a fork and soup spoon. The deep green escarole inspired me to serve it in pretty French stencilware shallow bowls.* **OPPOSITE** *All of the ingredients are prepared for hearty Turkey Meatball Soup with Escarole.*

LEFT *I plant amaryllis bulbs, which need seven to ten weeks to bloom, early in November to decorate the house during the holidays.* **OPPOSITE** *To my mind, these teacups and saucers are one of the most breathtaking patterns of Nippon lustreware—the perfect vessels for mouthwatering scoops of deep, dark Chocolate Sorbet.*

Chocolate Sorbet

3/4   *cup (packed) dark brown sugar*

1/2   *cup granulated sugar*

2/3   *cup unsweetened cocoa powder*

1   *ounce bittersweet chocolate, finely chopped*

2   *teaspoons pure vanilla extract*

SERVES 4

Combine 2½ cups water, brown sugar, granulated sugar, and cocoa in a saucepan. Bring to a boil over medium-high heat and cook, whisking occasionally, until the sugar dissolves, 4 or 5 minutes. Reduce the heat to low; boil gently for 3 minutes.

Meanwhile, set a medium bowl in an ice water bath. Remove the syrup from the heat and add the chocolate and vanilla; whisk until the chocolate is melted and well incorporated. Pour the mixture into the bowl over the ice water bath and stir occasionally until well chilled. Transfer to an ice cream maker and freeze according to the manufacturer's instructions.

MENU · MISO SOUP WITH ENOKI MUSHROOMS ·
SAKE-STEAMED SHRIMP ·
STEAMED MIZUNA · GREEN TEA ICE CREAM · SERVES 4

Most Japanese food is inherently low in fat, especially the dishes I like—sushi, oshitashi, pickles, steamed fish. A quick glance at this menu may give the impression that it is complicated. It is not. In fact, it relies on very simple cooking techniques, and the total cooking time is little more than 15 minutes. Be creative with your presentation, as is the Japanese way. Green tea ice cream can be purchased in Asian grocery stores. Cool sake, or masuzake, is often served in small cedarwood boxes with some salt piled in one corner and is drunk like tequila. I love to use the boxes in whimsical ways, and serving green tea ice cream in them is among my favorites. Of course, the ice cream is just as delicious in a pretty goblet or bowl.

Miso Soup with Enoki Mushrooms

1	4-inch square dried kombu, cleaned with a damp cloth
⅔	cup bonito flakes (fish flakes)
⅓	pound (1 package) enoki mushrooms, a few reserved for garnish
2	tablespoons miso
2	scallions, finely sliced

SERVES 4

In a pot, combine the kombu and water to cover and bring to a boil. Remove the kelp and discard. Add the bonito flakes, stir well, and remove from the heat. Let the flakes settle to the bottom of the pot. Strain the stock through a fine sieve, discarding the bonito flakes. Return the stock to the pot and add the mushrooms. Cook over moderate heat for about 3 minutes, or until the mushrooms have softened. In a small bowl, stir together a ladle of stock with the miso and stir the mixture into soup. Divide the soup among 4 bowls and sprinkle with the reserved enoki and the scallions.

Sake-Steamed Shrimp

1	cup sake
10	shiso leaves
20	medium shrimp, peeled and deveined
½	cup Sushi Rice (recipe follows)
4	tablespoons low-sodium soy sauce
4	teaspoons prepared wasabi paste

SERVES 4

In a large saucepan, combine the sake with 1 cup of water and 2 shiso leaves and bring to a boil. Reduce the heat and simmer. Add the shrimp and poach until light pink and the tails are curled, about 3 to 5 minutes.

For each serving, spread 2 tablespoons of Sushi Rice in a rectangle. Lay 2 shiso leaves on top and arrange 5 shrimp, tail end up, on the shiso leaves. Serve with 1 tablespoon soy sauce and 1 teaspoon wasabi paste.

Sushi Rice

1½	cups short- or medium-grain rice
3	tablespoons rice vinegar
1	tablespoon sugar
1½	teaspoons kosher salt

MAKES 3 CUPS

Place the rice in a bowl and gently rinse with cold water three or four times. Transfer to a strainer and let it rest for about 20 minutes.

Heat the vinegar, sugar, and salt in a nonreactive pan over medium heat, stirring until the sugar and salt are dissolved. Set aside.

Place the rice and 1½ cups of water in a saucepan. Simmer, cover, and cook over very low heat until the rice is tender and the water evaporates, about 20 minutes. Remove it from the heat, and let it rest, covered, for 20 minutes. Transfer the rice to a bowl, and toss with the vinegar mixture.

For each serving, spoon a ½ cup of rice into a small cylindrical container lined with plastic wrap. Turn the rice onto a plate, remove the wrap, and smooth the rice.

Steamed Mizuna

1	pound mizuna or other mild spicy green such as baby kale or arugula
	Kosher salt and freshly ground pepper

SERVES 4

In a large pot over high heat, bring 2 cups of water to a boil. Place the mizuna in a steamer basket, put in the pot, cover, and steam until wilted, about 3 minutes. Drain and squeeze out excess water. Add salt and pepper, mold into 12 squares, and divide among 4 plates.

Green Tea Ice Cream

1	pint green tea ice cream

SERVES 4

Spoon ½ cup of the ice cream into each of 4 cedarwood boxes and serve.

OPPOSITE *Cradle a bowl of Miso Soup with Enoki Mushrooms in your hands and sip the soul-warming broth straight from the bowl.*

LEFT *Shrimp steamed in sake and arranged on a shiso leaf draped over sushi rice, wilted mizuna shaped into pefect cubes, and slightly sweetened sushi rice shaped into a tall, smooth cylinder evoke the delicate pageantry with which Japanese food, no matter how simple, is served.* **ABOVE** *Cool sake is traditionally served in these cedar boxes, but I love to use the boxes as "bowls" for green tea ice cream.*

MENU · STOVE-TOP POTATOES · SAGE EGG-WHITE FRITTATA · MULLED CRANBERRY COCKTAIL · SERVES 4

Here is proof that an incredibly rich and flavorful frittata can be low in fat and very nutritious. Small whole sage leaves strewn about the whites make this especially perfect for a special Sunday brunch or unexpected midweek meal. I like to use the tiniest whole red potatoes I can find for the potato dish, but if they aren't available, simply quarter the larger ones. For this menu I serve the Mulled Cranberry Cocktail as a dessert, but I also love to drink it instead of tea on a freezing winter afternoon.

Stove-top Potatoes

8	small red potatoes
1	tablespoon extra-virgin olive oil
3	garlic cloves, thinly sliced
2	tablespoons chopped fresh parsley

SERVES 4

Place the potatoes in a skillet filled with water to cover. Add the oil and garlic, bring to a boil, and cook at a rolling boil until the water has evaporated, about 15 to 20 minutes. Cook the potatoes 2 to 3 minutes more, until the skins are seared and golden, stirring the potatoes with a wooden spoon once or twice. Divide among 4 plates and serve, sprinkled with parsley.

Sage Egg-White Frittata

9	egg whites
3	eggs
1	cup chanterelles, cleaned and chopped
	Kosher salt and freshly ground pepper
1	teaspoon extra-virgin olive oil or nonstick cooking spray
1/4	cup whole small sage leaves
2	cups mixed greens, trimmed, washed, and dried

SERVES 4

Preheat the oven to 375°F. In a bowl, whisk the egg whites until frothy. In another large bowl, whisk the eggs until foamy and lemon colored. Fold the egg whites into the eggs. Add the mushrooms and season with salt and pepper. Heat a nonstick ovenproof skillet slicked with olive oil or nonstick cooking spray over medium heat. Add the eggs, sprinkle the sage leaves on top, and cook for about 4 minutes, or until the edges are set. Transfer to the oven and cook for 4 to 6 minutes, until set and golden. Cut into wedges and serve over the mixed greens.

OPPOSITE *Pungent sage, nutty chanterelles, and the very freshest egg whites combine to make a delicious frittata. I usually set it on the dinner table on this enamel and iron griddle.*

Mulled Cranberry Cocktail

1	*quart cranberry juice*
1	*cinnamon stick*
2	*whole cloves*
$^1/_2$	*cup cranberries*
$^1/_2$	*cup sugar*
$^1/_4$	*teaspoon ground cinnamon*

MAKES 1 QUART

In a medium saucepan, combine the juice, cinnamon stick, and cloves and bring to a boil. Reduce the heat and simmer.

Meanwhile, in a small saucepan, combine the cranberries, sugar, ground cinnamon, and 2 tablespoons of water and heat over medium-low heat, gently stirring, until the cranberries pop and are well coated with the sugar mixture. When cool enough to handle, thread 3 to 4 berries each on 4 decorative toothpicks or skewers. Pour the mulled cranberry juice among 4 mugs and garnish with the cranberry swizzle.

LEFT *Stove-top Potatoes are cooked until the water boils off and then seared for a minute or two on the stovetop.* **ABOVE** *When I serve the frittata and potatoes for brunch, I like to make festive Mulled Cranberry Cocktail and serve it in my jadeite tea cups.*

MENU · PAN-SEARED PORK CHOPS ·
WARM WHEATBERRY SALAD ·
SPICY APPLESAUCE · PUMPKIN CUSTARD · SERVES 4

An updated, slimmed-down version of the classic pork chops and applesauce pairing, this menu will chase away the winter chill every time. I like to add hot red pepper flakes to my homemade sauce for a savory version. I also like to keep it on the slightly chunky side, especially when I serve it with a pilaf of wheatberries and mushrooms. Pumpkin Custard is essentially crustless pumpkin pie made with nonfat evaporated milk.

Pan-Seared Pork Chops

	Kosher salt and freshly ground black pepper
½	teaspoon dried thyme
4	pork chops, trimmed of fat (about 1 pound)
4	sprigs of fresh thyme
1	tablespoon extra-virgin olive oil
1	cup Chicken Stock (page 13) or low-sodium canned
1¼	cups marsala wine

SERVES 4

Combine the salt and pepper and dried thyme and rub on the pork chops. Press a sprig of thyme into each chop. Heat the olive oil in a nonstick skillet over medium-low heat and add the pork chops, thyme-side down. Sear 5 to 7 minutes per side, or until just browned and the interior is no longer bright pink. Transfer to a warm plate. Pour off the fat from the skillet, return to the heat, add the stock and wine, and bring to a boil. Reduce the heat and cook until slightly thickened, about 5 to 7 minutes. Spoon the sauce over the pork chops and serve.

Warm Wheatberry Salad

1	cup wheatberries
1	tablespoon extra-virgin olive oil
½	cup chopped white onions
1	cup sliced domestic mushrooms
½	cup white wine
2	teaspoons coarsely chopped parsley
2	teaspoons coarsely chopped sage
	Kosher salt and freshly ground black pepper

SERVES 4

Place the wheatberries in a strainer and rinse under cold water. In a large pot, combine the wheatberries in 2½ quarts of salted water and cook for 50 minutes, or until al dente. Drain and set aside.

Heat the olive oil in a skillet over low heat. Add the onions and cook until translucent, about 3 minutes. Stir in the mushrooms and add the white wine. Simmer for 10 minutes. Add the onions and mushrooms to the wheatberries in a medium bowl. Toss with the herbs, season with salt and pepper to taste, and serve warm.

LEFT *A fresh thyme sprig seared into a beautifully trimmed pork chop releases the most incredible aroma into the kitchen. I set the chop into the thickened pan juices and serve it with Spicy Apple Sauce.* RIGHT *Warm Wheatberry Salad flecked with onions, scallions, and mushrooms is a healthy alternative to rice pilaf.*

Spicy Applesauce

8 McIntosh apples, peeled, cored, and
      quartered
1 cup apple cider
½ teaspoon crushed red pepper
    Pinch of cayenne pepper
    Pinch of freshly ground black pepper

In a wide, heavy-bottomed saucepan, com-bine all of the ingredients and cook over medium heat, stirring often with a wooden spoon to prevent scorching, for 25 to 30 minutes, until the apples are broken down. Break apart the large pieces with the back of the spoon. Season with pepper and serve.

Pumpkin Custard

¾ cup canned pumpkin purée
2 large eggs
1½ cups evaporated skim milk
      (1 12-ounce can)
¾ teaspoon pure vanilla extract
½ cup (packed) light brown sugar
2 teaspoons cornstarch
½ teaspoon cinnamon
¼ teaspoon ground ginger
¼ teaspoon salt

SERVES 4

Preheat the oven to 350°F.

In a large bowl, whisk together the pump-kin, eggs, milk, and vanilla. In another bowl, stir together the brown sugar, cornstarch, spices, and salt and sift into the pumpkin mixture. Stir the batter until combined well and pour into four ¾-cup custard cups. Place the cups in a 9 × 11-inch baking pan and add enough warm water to come halfway up the sides of the cups. Bake for 50 minutes, or until set and browned lightly. Transfer the custards to a wire rack to cool.

MENU · ROASTED ROOT VEGETABLE RAGOUT · CREAMY POLENTA · PEAR MILK · GINGERSNAPS · SERVES 4

During the months when the produce aisle seems a bit bare—no locally grown tomatoes or piles of fresh corn in site—take advantage of the ever-growing variety of root vegetables that are showing up everywhere. Rough, rustic, and roasted, the root vegetables featured in this bistro menu are filling and comforting—and nutritious. Milk and cookies for dessert!

Roasted Root Vegetable Ragout

6	cipolline onions
4	baby turnips or 2 large, cut in eighths
1	small celery root, peeled and cut into wedges
½	pound whole baby carrots
3	new potatoes, halved
2	leeks, white part only, cleaned and cut into ¼-inch rings
2	parsnips, peeled and quartered
8	Brussels sprouts
1	tablespoon extra-virgin olive oil
2	sprigs each of fresh thyme, rosemary, and parsley
½	cup white wine
2	cups Vegetable Stock (page 13) or low-sodium canned
1	28-ounce can whole tomatoes
1	bay leaf
2	cups coarsely chopped Swiss chard
	Kosher salt and freshly ground black pepper
	Creamy Polenta (recipe follows)

SERVES 4

Preheat the oven to 475°F.

In a heavy roasting pan, combine the vegetables and olive oil and toss to coat. Roast 20 to 30 minutes, turning every 10 minutes, until the vegetables are nicely browned. Meanwhile, tie the herbs together with kitchen string. Transfer the pan to the top of the stove. Add the wine, stock, tomatoes, and herbs and cook over high heat for 15 minutes. Stir in the Swiss chard and cook 2 minutes more. Season with salt and pepper. To serve, spoon the vegetables and sauce over the polenta.

Creamy Polenta

4	cups Chicken Stock (page 13) or low-sodium canned
1	cup polenta
¼	cup skim milk
	Kosher salt and freshly ground black pepper

SERVES 4

In a large saucepan, bring the chicken stock to a rolling boil. Reduce the heat to medium and add the polenta slowly, whisking each addition very briskly. If the polenta is added too quickly, lumps will form. Cover and cook over low heat for 20 minutes or until the polenta is thick and creamy. Add the milk and stir to thoroughly incorporate. Season with salt and pepper and serve.

RIGHT *Winter vegetables glisten after a good roast in very high heat, which forces the concentration of their natural sugars.*

Pear Milk

2   cups skim or 1-percent milk
1   cup pear nectar
    Gingersnaps (recipe follows)

MAKES 3 CUPS

Fill four 6-ounce glasses with ice. Pour ½ cup milk and ¼ cup pear nectar into each and stir until blended. Serve each glass ice cold with 2 Gingersnaps.

Gingersnaps

1   cup plus 1 tablespoon all-purpose flour
1½   teaspoons baking soda
     Pinch of baking powder
     Pinch of kosher salt
¼   teaspoon cinnamon
1   teaspoon ground ginger
4   tablespoons (½ stick) unsalted butter, at
     room temperature
¾   cup sugar, plus some for sprinkling
1   large egg
¼   teaspoon pure vanilla extract
2   tablespoons molasses

MAKES 36 COOKIES

Sift together the flour, baking soda, baking powder, salt, cinnamon, and ginger. In a large bowl, combine the butter and sugar and mix on medium speed until the mixture holds together. Scrape down the sides of the bowl and add the egg, vanilla, and molasses. Mix on medium speed until incorporated. Add the dry ingredients to the bowl and mix until incorporated, about 1 minute.

Place the dough on parchment paper and roll out into an 8-inch-long × 1½-inch-wide log. Freeze until firm, up to 2 hours.

Preheat the oven to 350°F.

Slice the log into ¼-inch rounds, place on a baking sheet ½ inch apart, and sprinkle with sugar. Bake until the cookies crack slightly on the surface, about 12 minutes. Remove from the oven and let cool for 2 minutes on the baking sheet before transferring to a cooling rack.

ABOVE *The ultimate comfort meal, roasted vegetables tucked into creamy polenta warms chilled bones.* **OPPOSITE** *The combination of pear and ginger is among my favorites: I stir pear nectar into ice-cold milk and spike the cookie dough with fresh ginger.*

MENU · OPEN-FACED SEARED TUNA BURGER WITH
WASABI MAYONNAISE · TREVISO CAESAR SALAD ·
PASSION FRUIT SORBET · SERVES 4

Because these Seared Tuna Burgers are best eaten very rare, I strongly advise purchasing your sushi-quality tuna from a reputable fishmonger. The fish should be glistening and jewel-toned, with no trace of cloudiness. Wasabi paste, or Japanese horseradish, is distinctive not only for its bright green color, but also for its head-rushing heat. Combined with a little mayonnaise and low-fat sour cream, it becomes a perfect condiment for the tuna burgers. Wasabi is available in powder form, too, and can be mixed into a paste with a little water. I like setting the burger on the bottom half of a sourdough roll and eating the whole thing with a fork and knife. I use the top halves of the rolls to make croutons for the salad.

Open-faced Seared Tuna Burger with Wasabi Mayonnaise

1½	pounds sushi-quality tuna, coarsely chopped
	Kosher salt and freshly ground black pepper
¼	cup plus 1 tablespoon low-sodium soy sauce
3	tablespoons low-fat sour cream
1	tablespoon mayonnaise
2	teaspoons wasabi paste
4	sourdough rolls, bottoms only

SERVES 4

In a medium bowl, combine the tuna, salt and pepper, and 1 tablespoon of the soy sauce, and combine gently. Divide the mixture into 4 equal parts and shape each into a patty. Set aside. In a small bowl, combine the sour cream, mayonnaise, and wasabi paste. Stir to combine thoroughly and set aside.

Spray a large nonstick skillet with nonstick cooking spray and heat over medium-high heat. Add the tuna burgers and sear for 2 minutes on each side. Remove from the heat, add the soy sauce, return to the heat, and sear for 1 more minute per side. Place each on the bottom half of each roll, top with a tablespoon of dressing, and serve.

OPPOSITE *My winter version of a classic summer burger and salad, Open-faced Seared Tuna Burger with Treviso Caesar Salad is my favorite late-Saturday-afternoon meal. Rather than using the traditional romaine in my Caesar salads, I use spear-shaped and slightly bitter treviso, a close relative of radicchio.* **LEFT** *My earthenware egg cups are the perfect serving bowls for Passion Fruit Sorbet, which I scoop into fresh passion fruit halves.*

Treviso Caesar Salad

SOURDOUGH CROUTONS

4	sourdough rolls, tops only, cut into 1-inch cubes
2	teaspoons olive oil
1	tablespoon chopped fresh thyme
	Kosher salt

SALAD

1	small garlic clove, minced
2	tablespoons fresh lemon juice
1	tablespoon red wine vinegar
¼	teaspoon Dijon mustard
3	anchovy fillets, blotted and minced
2	tablespoons extra-virgin olive oil
	Kosher salt and freshly ground black pepper
2	heads treviso or radicchio, trimmed and torn into pieces
1	tablespoon freshly grated Parmigiano-Reggiano cheese

SERVES 4

Preheat the oven to 350°F.

In a small bowl, combine the sourdough pieces, olive oil, thyme, and salt and toss. Spread the croutons on a baking sheet and bake until golden, about 10 minutes, shaking the pan once or twice.

Meanwhile whisk the garlic, lemon juice, vinegar, mustard, and anchovies in the bottom of a large bowl. Gradually whisk in the olive oil. Season to taste with salt and pepper. Add the greens and toss to coat. Add the croutons and toss. Sprinkle with the cheese and serve.

Passion Fruit Sorbet

2	ripe passion fruit
1	pint passion fruit sorbet

Halve the passion fruit and set each in an egg cup or small bowl. Using a small ice cream scoop, scoop about ½ cup of the sorbet into each passion fruit half and serve.

211

MENU · GRILLED SARDINES OVER WILTED BABY ARUGULA · ORZO WITH PLUM TOMATOES AND OREGANO · MIXED CITRUS SALAD · SERVES 4

One of the most memorable weekends I have spent in my home in East Hampton happened to be in the dead of winter. After an especially invigorating walk on the beach, my friends and I visited my favorite local fishmonger to buy fish for dinner. He had fresh sardines in the case, which was quite unusual since they are not very easy to get. Buy them whenever you can find them, and prepare them simply—the way they are eaten all over the Mediterranean—tossed in olive oil and grilled to crispy golden-brown perfection. Be sure to cook your orzo al dente—if overcooked, the tiny rice-shaped pasta becomes mushy.

Grilled Sardines over Wilted Baby Arugula

2	large bunches of baby arugula, trimmed
16	fresh sardines, gills and innards removed
2	teaspoons extra-virgin olive oil
	Kosher salt and freshly ground black pepper
	Lemon wedges, for garnish

SERVES 4

Prepare a stove-top griddle or outdoor grill. Rinse the arugula, shaking off any excess water. Arrange on a large platter and set aside.

Rinse the sardines in cold water, rubbing to remove the scales. Wipe dry. In a bowl, combine the sardines and olive oil and toss to coat. Grill over very hot coals or heat about 2 to 3 minutes per side, or until the sardines are crispy and golden. Season with salt and pepper. Transfer immediately to the arugula-lined platter and serve with lemon wedges.

Orzo with Plum Tomatoes and Oregano

1	cup orzo
2	garlic cloves, slivered
1	tablespoon extra-virgin olive oil
2	plum tomatoes, seeded and coarsely chopped
1	tablespoon fresh oregano
1	tablespoon lemon juice
	Kosher salt and freshly ground black pepper

SERVES 4

In a large pot of boiling salted water, add the orzo and cook 10 to 12 minutes. Meanwhile, in a small saucepan over medium heat, combine the garlic and oil and cook 1 to 2 minutes. Using a slotted spoon, remove the garlic from the oil and discard. Remove the pan from the heat and add the tomatoes, oregano, and lemon juice. Set aside. Drain the orzo and transfer to a bowl. Add the tomato mixture and toss. Season with salt and pepper. Serve warm or at room temperature.

RIGHT *Iridescent sardines are best prepared simply—tossed in a little olive oil, grilled, and drenched in fresh lemon juice.*

Mixed Citrus Salad

4   blood oranges, peeled, downy
        membrane removed

1   large grapefruit, peeled, membrane
        removed, and sectioned

1   orange, peeled, membrane removed,
        and sectioned

4   black peppercorns, smashed
        underneath a heavy skillet

SERVES 4

Divide the fruit equally among 4 dessert
plates, season with pepper, and serve.

ABOVE *A painted steel French bistro table sets
the casual tone of this menu. Warm grilled sardines wilt and soften the arugula as they are
arranged over it. I like to spoon a bit of orzo
flecked with tomatoes and oregano onto my
plate and arrange the arugula and sardines
over it.* **RIGHT** *Toss the citrus sections in the
juices that collect as you peel and pith them.*

MENU · SAUTÉED RHUBARB CHARD ·
PUMPKIN THYME RIGATONI · A CHEESE TASTING · SERVES 4

This menu is one I return to again and again because I can prepare it in almost no time and it is truly satisfying. Any shaped pasta, such as penne, farfalle, and fusilli, are good substitutes for the rigatoni. Rhubarb chard, named for its brilliant red ribs, is delicious sautéed in a little olive oil and served on the side, but if you like, toss the sautéed greens into the pasta. Swiss chard, kale, dandelion greens, or sorrel can be substituted for the rhubarb chard. For dessert: a little taste of very high quality cheese. The cheese varieties I have selected for dessert are simply suggestions—they happen to be my favorites—and I encourage you to try these as well as to explore the hundreds of different cheeses available.

Sautéed Rhubarb Chard

2   *tablespoons extra-virgin olive oil*
3   *large garlic cloves, minced*
1½   *pounds rhubarb chard, stems trimmed and very coarsely chopped*
    Kosher salt and freshly ground black pepper

SERVES 4

In a large skillet over low heat, heat the olive oil. Add the garlic and sauté until the garlic begins to color, about 1 to 2 minutes.

Add the rhubarb chard and sauté until the leaves are just wilted, about 5 minutes. Season with salt and pepper.

Pumpkin Thyme Rigatoni

½   *pound rigatoni*
1   *teaspoon extra-virgin olive oil*
1   *medium-size onion, coarsely chopped*
¼   *cup brown sugar*
1   *small sugar pumpkin, peeled, seeded, and cut into chunks*
2   *cups Chicken Stock (page 13) or low-sodium canned*
1   *teaspoon cinnamon*
2   *teaspoons lemon juice*
2   *teaspoons thyme*
    Salt and freshly ground black pepper

In a large pot of boiling salted water, add the rigatoni and cook until al dente.

Meanwhile, in a nonstick skillet over medium heat, heat the oil. Add the onion and sauté until translucent, about 3 minutes. Add the sugar and stir until dissolved. Stir in the pumpkin. Add the chicken stock and reduce the heat to low. Cook until the sauce is thickened and the pumpkin is fork-tender. Add the cinnamon, lemon juice, thyme, and salt and pepper to taste. Toss in the pasta and serve.

A Cheese Tasting

4   *blood oranges, peeled, pith removed*
2   *ounces Reblochon*
2   *ounces Stilton*
2   *ounces Le Chevrot*

SERVES 4

Place a blood orange on each of 4 dessert plates. Divide each of the cheeses among the 4 plates and serve.

ABOVE LEFT *Once the heat hits rhubarb chard, the maroon veins brighten to an incredible fuchsia.* **ABOVE** *Spicy Stilton, nutty Reblochon, and creamy Le Chevrot are among my favorite cheeses. They make an exciting dessert when served with an exquisite blood orange on a white dish like this French creil creamware dessert plate.* **OPPOSITE** *Rigatoni is a great shape for trapping chunks of sugar pumpkin.*

217

MENU · SESAME SHRIMP · STEAMED SOYBEANS
WITH COARSE SALT · DASHI WITH SOBA NOODLES ·
ROSÉ GELATIN WITH BLACKBERRIES · SERVES 4

If one menu exemplifies the way I like to cook and eat now, this is it. To start, soybeans steamed and sprinkled with coarse salt. You can find the beans in the frozen section of most Asian markets. Sesame Shrimp, coated in fragrant sesame seeds and quickly seared in a tiny bit of sesame oil, are full of flavor and very low in fat. Perhaps the dish I make the most—each time varying it according to what I have in my pantry—is Dashi with Soba Noodles. Dashi is Japan's all-purpose stock, an almost ethereal broth infused with the subtle flavors of kombu (giant kelp) and bonito (dried fish flakes). Many supermarkets and all Asian markets carry both. Delicate yet filling soba noodles, made from buckwheat and wheat flour, together with beautifully julienned vegetables, make Dashi with Soba Noodles a perfect lunch on its own. Rather exotic looking, yet flavored perfectly for this menu, Rosé Gelatin with Blackberries is deceptively simple to make.

Sesame Shrimp

4	tablespoons sesame seeds
1–2	tablespoons dark sesame oil
1–2	tablespoons rice vinegar
2–3	tablespoons low-sodium soy sauce
12	large shrimp, peeled and deveined, tail portion of shell removed
4	6-inch bamboo skewers

SERVES 4

In a small skillet over medium heat, toast the sesame seeds until fragrant. In a shallow dish, combine 2 tablespoons of the sesame seeds with the sesame oil, vinegar, and soy sauce. Thread 3 shrimp onto each skewer, piercing each at the head and tail, and place in the marinade. Turn to coat and set aside for 10 minutes. Spread the remaining 2 tablespoons of sesame seeds on a plate. Transfer the skewers to the plate and coat with the sesame seeds. Heat the skillet over medium-high heat and sear the skewered shrimp for 2 to 3 minutes per side, or until opaque. Pour the remaining marinade over the shrimp and cook until the marinade thickens. Place the skewers on a plate and pour the marinade over. Serve warm or at room temperature.

Steamed Soybeans with Coarse Salt

1	pound fresh soybeans or 12 ounces frozen
	Kosher or sea salt
8	rice crackers

SERVES 4

In a pot of boiling water, add the soybeans and cook until bright green, about 5 minutes. Drain and refresh in cold water. Sprinkle with salt and serve with the rice crackers.

ABOVE *Sesame-crusted shrimp are seared in fragrant sesame oil.* **OPPOSITE** *Steamed soybeans, or edamame, are a popular starter in Asian restaurants, particularly in Japanese retaurants. I serve them with subtly sweet Japanese rice crackers.*

219

Dashi with Soba Noodles

1   strip kombu, about 7 inches long, wiped
       down with a damp cloth
¹/₂   cup bonito flakes (fish flakes)
2   tablespoons low-sodium soy sauce
3¹/₄   tablespoons mirin (Japanese rice wine)
       Juice of ¹/₄ lime
6   ounces soba noodles, cooked al dente
       and rinsed
1   small chayote, cut into fine julienne
1   medium carrot, peeled and cut into
       fine julienne
1   cup Kaiware sprouts
³/₄   cup enoki mushrooms
1   small daikon radish, peeled and cut into
       fine julienne
1   tablespoon freshly grated ginger,
       for garnish

SERVES 4

In a medium stockpot, combine 4 cups of
water and the kombu and bring to a boil.
Using a slotted spoon, remove the kombu.
Add the bonito flakes and remove the pot
from the heat. Allow the flakes to settle to
the bottom of the pot, and strain the broth.
Add the soy sauce, mirin, and lime juice.

Divide the noodles among 4 bowls.
Divide the vegetables evenly among the 4
bowls. Pour in the dashi, top each bowl with
a little grated ginger, and serve immediately.

Rosé Gelatin with Blackberries

1¹/₂   tablespoons unflavored gelatin (about
       1¹/₂ envelopes)
2   cups plus 1 tablespoon rosé wine
³/₄   cup plus 1¹/₂ tablespoons sugar
2   cups blackberries
1   tablespoon fresh lemon juice, strained

SERVES 4

In a large bowl, sprinkle the gelatin over 2
cups of cold water and let stand for 5 minutes to soften.

In a saucepan, bring 2 cups of wine, ³/₄ cup
of sugar, and 1 cup of blackberries to a boil.
Reduce the heat and simmer for 10 minutes.
Pour the hot wine mixture through a strainer
into the gelatin and discard the cooked
blackberries. Stir in the lemon juice and stir
the mixture until the gelatin is dissolved.

Place 1 blackberry in each of four ³/₄-cup
ramekins or custard cups and divide the
liquid among them. Chill the gelatins, covered, until set, about 5 hours.

In a small bowl, sprinkle the remaining
1¹/₂ tablespoons sugar over the remaining
blackberries. Add the remaining tablespoon of wine and toss to coat the berries.

Dip the bottom of each mold into a bowl
of warm water for 5 seconds and invert onto
chilled dessert plates. Spoon the blackberries around each gelatin and serve.

ABOVE *I was inspired to create this elegant
Rosé Gelatin with Blackberries by my love for
this kind of berry.* **OPPOSITE** *A French green
glazed earthenware bowl beautifully cradles
julienned vegetables that surround Dashi with
Soba Noodles.*

Rhubarb and Raspberries, Stewed, with a
    Meringue Crust, 22
Rice. *See also* Risotto; Wild Rice
    Saffron, 139
    Sticky, Gingered, 48
    Sushi, 195
Rice Pudding, 163
Ricotta with Ground Espresso, 50
Rigatoni, Pumpkin Thyme, 217
Risotto, Japanese, with Mushrooms and
    Scallions, 147
Risotto, Lemon, 21
Root Beer Float, 116
(root vegetable-beef) Pot-au-Feu, 175
Root Vegetable, Roasted, Ragout, 206
Rosé Gelatin with Blackberries, 221
Rutabagas, Mashed, 142

Saffron Rice, 139
Sage Egg-White Frittata, 199
Sake-Steamed Shrimp, 195
Salad
    Bean, Fresh, 114
    Cabbage Slaw, Double, 95
    Caesar, Treviso, 211
    Cherry Fruit, 121
    Chicories, Mixed with Warm Apple Thyme
        Dressing, 186
    Chopped, with Tarragon Vinaigrette, 68
    Citrus, Mixed, 214
    Endive, Arugula, and Tangerine, 24
    Endive, Curly, with Citrus Vinaigrette, 157
    Endive and Watercress, with Quick Pickled
        Red Onions, 129
    Escarole Hearts with Lemon Pumpkin Seed
        Vinaigrette, 137
    Farmstand with Grilled Turkey Sausage, 108
    Jicama Slaw, Cool, 77
    Layered Summer, 121
    Leafy Chopped, 100
    Lentil, Cold, 105
    Mixed Green, with Yellow Pepper
        Vinaigrette, 87
    Parsley Quinoa, 151
    Roasted Beet, 55
    Sprout and Daikon, Crunchy, with Mint, 165
    Tofu, with Soy-Ginger Dipping Sauce, 44
    Wheatberry, Warm, 202
Salmon, Smoked, Hot, 105
Salmon Trout, Poached, with Poppy Seed
    Vinaigrette, 50
Salsa Cruda, 91
Sandwich
    Burrito, Summer, 89
    Summer (tomato-avocado), My Favorite, 92
    (winter) Seared Tuna Burger, Open-faced, with
        Wasabi Mayonnaise, 211
Sardines, Grilled, over Wilted Baby Arugula, 212
Sauce, 14–15
    Arugula Pesto, 15
    Basil Pesto, Rough-Cut, 14
    Crème Fraîche, Enlightened, 14
    Dulce de Leche (sweet), 15
    Red Pepper Coulis, 15
    Salsa Cruda, 91
    Yogurt, Lemon Dill, 14

Scallops, Grilled, with Spring Greens, 21
Seafood Bouillabaisse, Curried Tomato, 139
Seafood, Calamari, Grilled Stuffed, 114
Sesame Shrimp, 219
Sesame Vinaigrette, 17
Shallots, Caramelized Corn with, 102
Shellfish. *See also* Clams; Crab; Mussels; Seafood;
        Scallops; Shrimp
    Stock, 13
Shortcake, Blueberry, 99
Shrimp
    Head-On, in Tomato Chervil Broth, 73
    Sake-Steamed, 195
    Sesame, 219
Slushes, Pink Margarita, 83
Smoked Salmon, Hot, 105
Snapper, Whole, Roasted, 183
Soba Noodles, Dashi with, 221
Sorbet, Chocolate, 193
Sorbet, Passion Fruit, 211
Soufflé, Lime, 64
Soup. *See also* Stock
    Beef Barley, 55
    Broth, Hot and Sour, with Shredded
        Chicken, 48
    Buttermilk Tomatillo, Chilled, 89
    Butternut Squash, with Roasted Garlic, 169
    Chicken, The Very Best, 186
    Corn Chowder, 108
    Cucumber and Dill, Cool, 80
    Eggplant, Charred, with a Red Pepper
        Swirl, 153
    Miso, with Enoki Mushrooms, 195
    Pea, Bright Green, 29
    Seven-Onion, 157
    Turkey Meatball, with Escarole and
        Papparelle, 191
    Wild Mushroom, 42
Sourdough Bread, Crusty, with Parsley Pesto, 188
Soy-Ginger Dipping Sauce, 44
Soybeans, Steamed, with Coarse Salt, 219
Spaghetti Squash with Sage and Orange, 34
Spice-Rubbed Roast Pork Loin, 165
Spinach, Steamed Baby, 132
Spring Greens, Grilled Scallops with, 21
Sprout, Crunchy, and Daikon Salad with
    Mint, 165
Squash, Butternut, Soup with Roasted Garlic, 169
Squash, Spaghetti, with Sage and Orange, 34
Star Fruit, Broiled, in Gingered Broth, 170
Sticky Rice, Gingered, 48
Stock
    Beef, 14
    Chicken, 13
    Lamb, 14
    Shellfish, 13
    Vegetable, 13
Strawberries and Vanilla Syrup, 42
Striped Bass, Herbed, 132
Succotash, Corn, Fava Bean and Cucumber, 58
Sugar Snap Peas with Mint Leaves, 96
Summer Burrito, 89
Summer Sandwich (tomato-avocado), My
    Favorite, 92
Sushi, Fruit, Cold, with Honey Dipping
    Sauce, 148
Sushi Rice, 195

Sweet Potatoes, Roasted, with Pineapple
    Cranberry Chutney, 137
Swiss Meringue, 22
Swordfish Kebabs, Yogurt-Marinated, 154

Tarragon Vinaigrette, 16
Tart, Lemon, Thin, 167
Thyme-Roasted Poussin, 129
Tofu Salad, Cold with Soy-Ginger Dipping
    Sauce, 44
Tomatillo Buttermilk Soup, Chilled, 89
Tomato(es)
    Compote, Raw, Grilled Artichokes with, 41
    Chervil Broth, Head-On Shrimp in, 73
    Cipolline Compote, Chunky, 180
    with Orrechiette, 96
    Plum, Orzo with, and Oregano, 212
    Seafood Bouillabaisse, Curried, 139
Tortillas, Corn, Warm, 38
Treviso Caesar Salad, 211
Tuna Burger, Open-faced Seared, with Wasabi
    Mayonnaise, 211
Tuna Steak, Grilled, 24
Turkey Meatball Soup with Escarole and
    Papparelle, 191
Turkey Sausage, Grilled, Farmstand Salad
    with, 108

Vegetable. *See also* Name of Vegetable
    Handrolls (nori), 47
    Ragout, Roasted Root, 206
    Stock, 13
Venison, Roasted Rack of, with Pomegranate
    Sauce, 142
Vinaigrette, 16–17
    Dill Shallot, 16
    Chive, 17
    Citrus, 17
    Jalapeño, 17
    Lime Caper, 17
    Orange, 17
    Poppy Seed, 17
    Red Pepper, 16
    Sesame, 17
    Tarragon, 16
    Yellow Pepper, Raw, 16

Watercress and Endive Salad with Quick Pickled
    Red Onions, 129
Watermelon Squares in Campari, 95
Wheatberry Salad, Warm, 202
Wild Mushrooms
    Enoki, Miso Soup with, 195
    Morels, Sauteed, 63
    Portobello Pizzas, Grilled, 85
    Soup, 42
Wild Rice with Dried Fruit, 129

Yellow Pepper, Raw, Vinaigrette, 16
Yogurt
    Cheese, 15; Grilled Fruit Panini with, 102
    Cones with Kiwis, 78
    Frozen, with Pink Peppercorns, 137
    -Marinated Swordfish Kebabs, 154
    Sauce, Lemon Dill, 14